In Memoriam: McAfee Remembered

WHACKD

Published by WHACKD, 2024.

IN MEMORIAM: MCAFEE REMEMBERED

First edition. November 18, 2024.

Copyright © 2024 WHACKD.

ISBN: 978-1739365028

Written by WHACKD.

Table of Contents

"Getting subtle messages from U.S. officials saying, in effect: "We're coming for you McAfee! We're going to kill yourself". I got a tattoo today just in case. If I suicide myself, I didn't. I was WHACKD. Check my right arm."

- John McAfee

"I am content in here. I have friends. The food is good. All is well. Know that if i hang myself, a la Epstein, it will be no fault of mine."

- John McAfee

Prologue

WHACKD presents 'In Memoriam: McAfee Remembered,' a tribute to John McAfee's life and legacy. This book features intimate interviews with John's former associates, friends, and widow Janice McAfee, giving personal insight into the life of the late British-American computer programmer and leading authority on internet security, privacy, and hacking.

John founded McAfee Associates in 1987, revolutionizing computers with the world's first anti-virus software. Under his leadership the company helped establish best practices for computer security with new malware detection and removal approaches. McAfee resigned from the cybersecurity firm in 1994 with an estimated $100 million, after profiting from its stock market flotation. In a testament to its success, Intel acquired the company for an impressive $7.68 billion in 2010. Although John later voiced criticisms of the software, labelling it as both ineffective and intrusive, his profound influence on the cybersecurity landscape remains indisputable and continues to shape the field today.

McAfee founded many revolutionary companies during his life, another being Tribal Voice, one of the worlds first internet chat programs for Windows. The software had advanced features like Voice-over-internet-protocol, whiteboard, speech synthesizer, and web sharing. But AOL sued them and blocked interoperability with their client. Tribal Voice was later bought by CMGI and ceased operations in 2002.

Another was QuorumEx, a biotech firm in Belize, that aimed to make antibiotics from native plants. John stated his company found a natural substance that could kill bacteria by disrupting their communication, known as 'quorum sensing.' QuorumEx was part of

WHACKD

McAfee's vision to create innovative and disruptive technologies that could challenge the status quo and have a positive impact on the world.

~~~

John believed in the transformative power of cryptocurrency and was actively involved in the cryptocurrency space, promoting, launching, and overseeing various projects. Notably, he became the CEO of MGT Capital Investments in 2016, a company focused on cybersecurity and cryptocurrency mining.

In 2019, he founded WHACKD, a cryptocurrency designed to raise awareness about the Jeffrey Epstein scandal. Through this project, John sought to provide a social commentary that linked political assassination with the dynamic world of meme culture, all securely archived on the blockchain. John also strongly advocated that privacy is a fundamental human right which led him to launch GHOST, a privacy-focused blockchain project that he saw as a crucial tool in fighting against government overreach.

The significance of these projects lies in McAfee's vision of creating a decentralized environment, where users can communicate and transact without intermediaries or authorities, empowering people to reclaim their sovereignty and freedom using blockchain technology to convey ideas and solutions.

In addition to his business ventures, McAfee was a prominent political figure who ran for president of the United States twice, seeking the Libertarian Party nomination in 2016 and 2020. Throughout his efforts, he aimed to bring his unique perspective and vision to the national stage, advocating fiercely for individual liberty and freedom.
~~~

IN MEMORIAM: MCAFEE REMEMBERED

He was a controversial figure known for his diverse pursuits as a cryptocurrency promoter, political activist, and fugitive. With a lifestyle that embraced yoga, drugs, guns, and sex, he became a larger-than-life character, navigating a tumultuous path marked by legal troubles that spanned from Tennessee all the way to Central America and the Caribbean.

<center>~~~</center>

John's final downfall came after the IRS indicted him, his wife, and his campaign staff on felony tax charges. This led to further charges from the U.S. Department of Justice for failing to file tax returns spanning several years. During that time, McAfee is accused of earning millions from various ventures, including consulting, speaking engagements, cryptocurrencies, and selling the rights to his life story. He was additionally accused of hiding assets like a yacht, cars, bikes, and real estate by transferring them into other people's names.

In January 2019, before his eventual arrest, John and his wife fled the United States on a million-pound yacht. Accompanying them were a couple of ex-military security guards, several high-powered rifles, a variety of other firearms, and their dogs, as they sailed to the Bahamas and other Caribbean destinations. John maintained a strong presence on social media during this time, tweeting about his adventures and seemingly carefree lifestyle. He even ran his 2020 presidential campaign from international waters, in exile, while evading law enforcement.

After a long cat-and-mouse game, John was arrested at an airport in Barcelona in October 2020, as he was trying to board a flight. He spent the next eight months in the Brians 2 prison where he posted several messages on his Twitter account stating that he was being persecuted by the US government and that he had no intention of killing himself. During this period John was facing the possibility of extradition to the United States.

On the day of his death, June 23rd 2021, the Spanish National Court dismissed John's claim that he faced political persecution and inhumane treatment if he was forced to return to the US, and they rejected his appeal against the extradition. Hours later, John McAfee was reportedly found dead in a Barcelona prison. He was 75 years old and had been detained in Barcelona for 8 months and 20 days, since October 4th 2020.

Following John's death, conspiracy theories and speculation surged online, fuelled by his cryptic Twitter posts and statements from his lawyer and widow, Janice McAfee, who insisted he was not suicidal and demanded answers from authorities.

Compounding this turmoil, the "WHACKD" token—originally launched by John, meant as a satirical commentary on the death of Jeffrey Epstein—saw a significant influx of liquidity as supporters traded it in high volume. Online pages appeared with countdown timers to hypothetical events, seeking to exploit the situation for personal gain. Many believed the token was intrinsically linked to a 'Dead Mans Switch,' further fuelling speculation about its value and the mysterious circumstances surrounding his passing.

~~~

During the conducting of interviews for this book, Spanish authorities retained John's remains within a Barcelona morgue, where the official autopsy had taken place. They deprived his widow of the opportunity to seek an independent autopsy and withheld vital documents, including the death certificate, toxicology report,
~~~

and the official autopsy findings, preventing her from carrying out the necessary steps regarding his final arrangements.

As this print edition is published, Spanish authorities have finally released John's remains on December 14, 2023, after a 904-day campaign spearheaded by his widow, Janice McAfee. Throughout this arduous journey, Janice stayed in Spain, passionately advocating not only for the return of John's remains but also for the issuance of a death certificate, toxicology report, and official autopsy findings. Despite her unwavering determination, the Barcelona courts have refused to authorize the release of the autopsy report. John was cremated as per his wishes.

This collective portrayal offers readers an exclusive, nuanced understanding of John as seen through the eyes of his closest friends, family, and colleagues, providing a genuine insight into his character, passions, and motivations that have shaped his legacy. We are grateful to John's loved ones and associates for sharing their personal experiences and recollections with us, and we hope that this book accurately reflects their relationship with the late tech innovator.

Through the stories of those who knew him, this book celebrates the legacy of a man who dared to dream big and live life on his terms, inspiring others to do the same.

Chapter One
Janice McAfee

WHACKD – Hi Janice, thank you for doing this. Please introduce yourself and tell me about the night you first met John McAfee?

Janice McAfee – My name is Janice McAfee and I met John, I believe it was December 2012, it was the day after he was deported from Guatemala after the whole situation in Belize.

When we met, I was working as a prostitute in South Beach, Miami. Before I met John, I had been a prostitute for the previous nine years, and so I was with another working girl that night. We were hanging out at the Mango's Café, which is more like a bar in the night time, with a dance floor and all that stuff. I had decided me and my girlfriend were going to go hang out at the Hard Rock Casino in Fort Lauderdale. My car happened to be parked across from the hotel where John was staying, which was the Beacon Hotel, on Ocean Drive.

As we're walking to our car, I see John standing in front of Johnny Rockets with one of the workers there talking to him. As I walked by, I size him up as a potential client, he looked pretty rough and straggly so I made the incorrect assumption that he was broke, but I did make the correct assumption that he wasn't interested in being entertained for the evening.

But we met eyes and we smiled at each other, he nodded back as I continued walking and I just happened to turn and look back around as I caught him looking at my butt, he kind of smiled sheepishly and I continued on my way.

IN MEMORIAM: MCAFEE REMEMBERED

As I got to the hotel the night security was on site, I'd spoken to him many times before just to see what was happening in the night: "Who's in town?" "What parties are in town?" "What cops are out harassing girls tonight?" and so we're having a similar conversation. He looked down the street towards where John was standing, and said "You know who that is right? Do you know McAfee Antivirus? Well, that's the creator of it." So, I just said, "Fuck it, what's the worst that can happen?" My girlfriend and I ran down the street and we caught up with him in front of the News Café, again on Ocean Drive.

When I caught up with him, he was smoking a cigarette, I asked him if I could have one, and while he was lighting it for me, he asked "So, what are you girls doing out here, drugging and rolling old men?" I told him "We don't use drugs." Then I went into my spiel, you know: "You want to date? Are you looking for some company? You can have a two-for-one. Do you like chocolate or do you like vanilla?" Just to get that out of the way, but as I had guessed, he wasn't interested.

He said that he'd had one hell of a journey and all he wanted was a cup of coffee, then he surprised me by asking us if we wanted to join him. We sat down and ordered coffee and I asked him who he was and if he was there for business or pleasure, he was kind of taken aback by that. He had been at the top of the news for months. It was an international story about him hiding, being on the run in South America, and then being deported. I had no idea about that at the time because I didn't watch the news, so I didn't know what had been going on and he was very much surprised by that.

We spent the next three hours just talking to each other. He shared what details he wanted to about what happened in Belize and the circumstances that brought him to Miami. After about three hours he asked me to get rid of my girlfriend because she was high on MDMA and not adding much to the conversation, so I asked her to leave. Then he asked me to stay the night with him, it was morning by that time, maybe four a.m., but what was left of the night he asked me to spend with him. So, we get to his hotel and he very boyishly asked me if we could just cuddle. I was like "Yeah sure." Me being a working girl, I thought when he said cuddle, he was meaning some kind of kinky or sexual thing. I didn't know what it was, but I was sure that I could figure out how to perform it well. But all he genuinely wanted was a cuddle, an actual cuddle. He got in bed, laid his head on my shoulder, and within five minutes he was asleep. It was sweet, I also had the best sleep of my life at that time, so it was a good night.

WHACKD – In retrospect, what do you make of John's Belize saga, the Laboratory, the story of officials extorting him, the murder of his neighbour Gregory Faull, and the alleged keystroke logging software on donated computers?

Janice McAfee – I didn't know about any of that at the time, but in retrospect, I believe what he said was one hundred percent true because of everything that happened during our time together. People would come after him. There was a constant threat of danger throughout our relationship.

And so, a little about my situation: I had a pimp when first I met John. My pimp was later approached by a cartel representative, who then sent that same representative to me. My pimp was paid $50,000, and he gave the cartel assurances that he would get me to cooperate as their 'inside man'. I was threatened, my family was threatened, and my children were threatened. If I didn't cooperate, they would be brutally murdered.

IN MEMORIAM: MCAFEE REMEMBERED

I was stuck in a situation where I felt like I couldn't trust anyone, not even John, to say what was happening. I didn't think he could or would protect me. Protecting my children was my job. Whatever I could do to protect them I was going to do. So, I planned to give them the illusion that I was cooperating with them on whatever they were asking me to do. I would have to tell them stuff like: "I can't do it, John's watching me." I pretended that I wasn't able to perform whatever tasks they were asking me to do, and I was able to dance that dance for a while. At the same time, I was trying to warn John of how he needed to protect himself from the things that they were telling me to do or from the things that I had heard them talking about planning to do to him.

An example of that: I drove John around a lot, we were living in Portland at the time and whenever we went out John was on his phone, always busy with something, so I would drive us to wherever we had to go. Knowing that, they asked me to park John's truck on the street so they would have access to it, to disable it or booby-trap it or something, I'm not sure what, but after that, I started parking it in the parking garage of our flat, it had the perfect parking space so I told John to do the same thing, you know: "Don't leave it on the street."

I would be out of town frequently to see my children, so I would travel on a short flight from Portland to California to see them. I would always say to them "Don't go out at night by yourself, make sure someone drives you around. Don't park the car in the street, go park it in the parking garage."

That was kind of my way of warning John or at least telling him to notice what was happening. But I didn't need to tell him any of that, because he already knew everything that was happening, in real-time. He knew about the pimp, and he knew about the cartel representative. Looking back in hindsight, I know that for sure. At the time I would assume it because he would say certain things, or he would do things that would let me know that he was probably aware of what was happening. But I didn't trust him at the time. Some things happened between John and me, fights and stuff, that unfortunately made this situation with the pimp drag out an awful lot longer than it should have. I didn't know who around us was part of what the pimp and the cartel representative were doing, or who else had their own agenda going because there was a lot of that happening too.

A lot of people who came around John, that we had in our personal space, were not good. They were seeking to do John harm, in whatever way, whether it was physical, financial, reporting on John's movements and whereabouts, or whatever else. As I said, there was a constant threat of danger around us, always, throughout our relationship. So, I believe John's account of the situation in Belize.

Something that people may not know from that period in Belize is that it wasn't just one dog of his that was poisoned, there were nine of his dogs poisoned. Now, these dogs were not all John's. He said he brought two or three dogs to Belize from Colorado but he had 25 dogs all together in Belize, they were mostly strays. They somehow found where he was staying and with him being an animal lover, especially a dog lover, he wouldn't turn them away. So, in that sense, they became his dogs, and so people were complaining. But they weren't his dogs, they belonged to whoever left their dogs or let them roam.

But, nine of them were poisoned, he told me that story the night I met him. As a way of mercy, he had to shoot all nine dogs because they were vomiting and had blood coming from their mouths and their rectums, they were in agony.

WHACKD – I remember John saying that was the most painful thing he ever experienced in his life.

Janice McAfee – Yeah, can you imagine? Nine of your animals... This is why he felt that it wasn't his neighbour that did this, but that it was the government of Belize, this is what he said to me. He said "Someone from within the government has done this to my dogs," because so many of them were poisoned. He also said he wasn't aware of any complaint that his neighbour had filed and that the neighbours complaining about dogs were not an infrequent thing because they were loud and they barked at people, but they weren't technically his dogs. He did his best to try to keep them well-behaved and from harassing the neighbours. He also believed that his neighbour's murder may have been a botched attempt on his own life, perhaps hitmen went to the wrong house. That's what John believed.

WHACKD – What events occurred in John's life in Belize before the murder of his neighbour?

Janice McAfee – John was working on topical anti-virus research, the plant that he was using to make it could only be found there, it was a specific plant that was native to the jungle and so they were trying out these medicinal sprays. He had the idea because he was getting crazy insect bites over there. When he first came back to Miami, he had these old bite marks all over his legs and his arms, he evidently didn't wear long sleeves or long pants, but this was why he came up with the idea. It was a way to relieve that problem, not just for himself but also for the people on the island, as they all had to deal with these things too. So, he tried it out, he made samples and he started giving them out, he was working to help people.

Then he said that two representatives from the government went to visit him at his property, and they asked him if he would consider donating. I don't know if it was to a specific official, or just in general to a political party. Either way, it was suggested to him that it would make his life easier if he did so. In return, he would receive certain perks there in Belize: women, land and whatever else he may have been looking for. John said "No thank you, I'm not interested", you know, no big deal.

About a week later, there was a raid on his property and they left him with half a million dollars worth of damage in his lab and accusations of a meth lab. He was working on topical antibiotics and anti-viral sprays; it certainly wasn't a meth lab. I'm not sure how that rumour even started, it's a crazy rumour if you think about it for a moment. A gringo, someone who was never been in the drug trade, all of a sudden decides they want to become a drug lord in Belize? Where the cartels and other nefarious organisations have a foothold in the drug trade, and this lone gringo is just going to come in and infringe on the territory like that? It's crazy.

But, during the raid, they not only destroyed the lab, but they also killed one of his dogs. It was one of his favourite dogs. This dog was deaf, and he loved John.

The dog had come round and he saw John kneeling on the ground so he started innocently running up to him, then one of the armed men said "If you think we're not serious," and then shot the dog right there and then. The dog lay there dead as John was on the floor in handcuffs, with all of the workers also kneeling on the dirt, in handcuffs. John said they were there like that for nearly 14 hours.

A couple of days later, one of the government representatives returned to speak with John and asked him if he had reconsidered his donation, to which John responded "Get the fuck off my property before I pull out my pistol and shoot you in the head." It was probably there that he had the idea to try to collect evidence if he hadn't been thinking about it already.

Then the Belizean government received these laptops from John, as a donation, but they were loaded with keystroke-logging software and John was collecting all of the data. He said he hired some girls to listen to the conversations and alert him when his name was mentioned or any other things that were important to him, so that's what they were monitoring for. Then he said they found out about human trafficking, drug trafficking, money laundering and all sorts of nefarious activities, involving not only the Belizean officials but also their US counterparts. He said some very well-known people within our government were involved with these activities.

John's operation was later exposed after one of the girls John had hired to parse that information was sleeping with a man within the police or the GSU, I'm not sure which exactly. But, one of the girls was sleeping with this official and during pillow talk, she outed the whole thing to him, like: "We're doing this for John McAfee, he's got these computers and they're listening to people," and this spread very quickly throughout the political apparatus. So now John had this huge problem and he needed to go into hiding. He had a place in San Pedro, and he had Samantha with him, so he would hide out there a lot of the time. At the time of the murder, he had been in hiding around the island from the government officials already, and whomever their muscle was. I think he said it was the GSU. In Belize, they are the guys the officials use when they have a problem that they want to be solved on the island.

So, John had been in hiding since about the summer of that year in 2012. His neighbour was murdered in November, but from the summer up until November, John had been already in hiding because he had already been exposed to the people he was spying on. He had given keystroke logging laptops to various secretaries that worked for high-up officials within the Belizean government and he did this in the hope of finding evidence that they had set him up for the raid in the summer of 2012.

So, that is all he was initially looking for, he wasn't looking for everything else that he found out later, he found a lot of that tough. He was dealing with this the whole time and then everything goes international after his neighbour died. They tried to put that on him when they wanted to question him but he was never a suspect or suspected of murdering his neighbour, he was only a person of interest.

When John got back to America, he offered numerous times for the Belizean authorities to come and question him there. If all they wanted to do was question him then that could have happened anywhere. It could have happened when he was back in Miami after he was deported. There was no need for him to go back to Belize, it just wasn't necessary if all they honestly wanted was to ask him questions, which we knew wasn't true.

WHACKD – When John returned to the U.S. from Belize in 2012, you both eventually moved to Portland and John began to reinvent himself, you both created a parody video with guns, girls and bath salts, talking shit about the antivirus company that made him millions. Can you share any little-known stories from that time?

Janice McAfee – So, the thing about the video, he was getting slammed a lot on Twitter whenever he posted and people were constantly associating him with the antivirus, which was a common occurrence back then. It still happens now but it used to be a lot more frequent. So, he was getting trashed a lot about the McAfee Anti-Virus and so he decided to create a video taking all the negative headlines about himself and putting the spotlight on them all in one video. The bath salts in the video were corn starch. I know because I snorted it.

But, those couple of days were so much fun though, he would read comments from people off the internet about the problems they were having with the antivirus software, as there were still people complaining to him about it, so he used that as a part of the video. It was a lot of fun, working on this collaborative effort to make it as viral as it is now.

WHACKD – When John moved back to the US from Belize, he started participating in keynote speeches on topics of cybersecurity and, later, cryptocurrency across America. What was that time like for you?

Janice McAfee – Travelling with John while he was doing those keynotes were the happier times for me. I could turn my phone off and go months sometimes without talking to my pimp or having to deal with the stress of it all. I was able to put it right out of my mind and feel sort of free like I could breathe a little bit.

Also watching John, he was so brilliant, the absolute genius that he was. Just watching him give these talks that he never prepared for, he never wrote notes, he never really knew what he was going to say until he got up there. He never practised; he would just speak from the heart.

He told me he would decide as he was walking up on stage what he was going to speak about. He looks at the audience and then assesses what he feels he should share with them. Whether it was for cybersecurity, crypto or whatever other various talks he was doing around those times, he would speak from his heart, and it was always full of wisdom. I was always fascinated watching him.

I remember asking him if he ever got nervous when he was up on stage, and he was like "Fuck yes, I get so nervous." At that time, he would have his hand in his pocket and when I would do his laundry, I would always find this balled-up money, or paper or whatever was in his pocket. It would be balled up; when he was nervous that was his self-soothe until he was comfortable, and then he became more animated with his hands and arms.

He enjoyed taking questions from the audience and he enjoyed talking to people individually. After the conferences, he would spend over an hour meeting and greeting people, and taking pictures. People would ask him questions and he would take whatever time necessary to answer them. He wanted to interact with people and it was just great to watch that.

WHACKD – What dangers did you both face during that time?

Janice McAfee – During that time, the Cartel Representative I mentioned was around and he is someone that John knew. I will give you his name, but I don't know if I want it to be a part of your book. It's a man that came to me, the man that approached my pimp.

I haven't spoken about this since John died, I guess my hesitancy is about whether or not I want to make any more enemies or reignite... whatever.

So anyways, his name is XXXXXXXX XXXXXX and he's the same man who runs XXXXX XXXXX. John knew who he was, but John is the type of person who brought his enemies in. He never let on to them that he knew who they were, or that he knew what they were about, and he did that masterfully.

He would bring in his enemies as close as he could, and watch them to learn what they were doing, he believed in that. I didn't realise at the time he was just bringing his enemies in, because it looked to me like there was a genuine relationship there. Maybe there might have been, maybe not. John might have been using it for whatever reason, but to me, it just looked strange.

I'm not willing to take that risk, I don't have the knowledge John had when it comes to cyber-security. He's able to get the goods, whereas I have to look at someone and make my assessment just by looking at them. If this person is a threat to me, then I'm gonna keep them away or minimise my interactions at least. John was the opposite; he would bring them in to watch them.

So, that was happening consequently and XXXXXXXX would bring people in. He was bringing in directors to film John, and to travel with us for a documentary. There was also going to be a book and so XXXXXXXX brought in a writer. I assumed the people he brought in were also part of this plot to bring John harm. I don't know why they wanted him; I just knew that the cartel wanted him and that's never good. I also knew they operate around South America, Belize being a part of the area with ties to that stuff, but the cartels run free in America. Different cartels work within different parts of the country. The Sinaloa Cartel is who XXXXXXXX was a representative of, they have footholds in Florida, California, Arizona, and all over the place.

Initially, I was only told that they wanted to use me to get information about John. I was extremely vocal about not doing this or that, you know: "This is dangerous," "You're gonna get me killed." It quickly became more and more things, like: "Hide his guns" or "Get us a spare key to the apartment." They had also given me a grainy substance that they wanted me to cook into his food... All things that I didn't do, but with all these different people around John, it just made it more difficult for me to find a way to tell him what was happening. And, I just didn't feel safe telling him.

I was concerned that it would somehow get back to my pimp or XXXXXXXX, as then something would immediately happen to my family, which was always a major concern for me.

WHACKD – You and John later moved to Tennessee in 2014 and then John later went on to run for the 2016 presidential election, what are your highlights from that period and what dangers did you face during that time?

Janice McAfee – So, the pimp found out that I moved with John to Tennessee, we first moved there in 2014. We got our first house in Tennessee in 2015, but we were there in the summer of 2014 as we were living with John's head of security at the time. His name was John Pool.

We were living with them in their family home for a couple of months. Pool's partner lived there and she had young children. John didn't want to bring any danger and he was concerned that something would happen, so after we had been staying there for a couple of months we decided to leave. John didn't want to put them in harm's way, so we left and went on a road trip and I got to see Niagara Falls with him and we stayed in different various hotels along the way. It was cool, but it was very cold. Then we started looking for a place to buy because I found out that the pimp was already there in Jackson, Tennessee and had a house there, so now I had that problem. I have no idea how the fuck he found out that we were in Tennessee.

I will mention this too, we were living in Colorado before that and I don't remember if John was in town at the time because he had his 'flavours of the week' so I would be home alone sometimes with our dogs. We had Tequila, the red-nose Pitbull and we also had a puppy, a blue-nose Pitbull called Jack Daniels, we called him JD. I don't know why we were naming our dogs after liquor, but we were. One day I went to the store for some things and as I come out of the store my pimp is standing next to my car. I still cannot figure out how the fuck he knew I was in the store at that moment. I still don't know how the fuck he was able to be there as I came out of the store. That scared the shit out of me.

So, there were things like that which made me think there was far more to the situation than whatever my pimp was involved in. Many more moving parts were all vested in collecting John, so this was the danger as it presented itself later on in Tennessee.

I eventually came clean with John about everything when we went to Europe, I told him everything about XXXXXXXX, about various other people that I either knew were involved, or that I thought were involved because of their relationship with XXXXXXXX, and because of the different plots and the things that they were asking me to do.

When the pimp came to Tennessee, I don't know why I didn't tell John, I was just afraid that he wouldn't believe me, or that he wouldn't believe that I wasn't involved with whatever they were plotting, I don't know. I just didn't tell anyone about it. Then again, I didn't need to because John already knew.

We went house hunting one time, just looking for places to live, he drove to where the pimp's house was and that was like, "Fuck, he knows, he really knows." Again, I don't know why I didn't tell him at the time, I just was afraid to, but he let me know that he knew. Once we moved into our home there were some other situations. As I said, John liked to bring his enemies in close, so he would hire people to do work around the house and maybe also as a way to keep an eye on them or an eye on me. There was always something happening around us. Once people knew where we lived there was even more concern for our safety. At the time John had bought a home for his head of security in the same town. That was in Lexington, about a ten-minute drive from where we settled and found a home: 'The Tree House' in Lexington, Circle Drive, Tennessee.

We had security cameras set up and after John thought that someone was trying to break into the house, he installed booby traps around the front of the house and in the bushes. The house looked like a real tree house. You can look it up online, the address was 79 Circle Drive, I believe. You can look at the house and see why I call it 'The Tree House.' It was a cool place. So, at the front of the house, there were these bushes that John booby-trapped with fishing lines and these big fish hooks. Well, someone got caught in them one night and had to pull off the whole branch as they couldn't get out of the fish hooks. John came back to the house and saw the broken branch where the hooks were, so obviously, something had happened there, quite clearly, so we would stay up some nights, just watching and listening, it was very stressful.

We also had some people stay that were not really on the up and up. Again, this was someone that John had invited into our space, so that was an issue as well. But it helped to have extra bodies in the house if it helped deter whatever was happening externally, but it was a very complicated and chaotic time.

WHACKD – Following the end of the first election in 2016, it seemed to be a wild period, it was later reported that John went on a naked shooting spree inside the house. Can you share what that time was like?

Janice McAfee – Okay, so he decides to run for president in 2015, and he decided to create 'The Cyber Party'. At the time he was also working with people in Alabama to create a tech hub of some kind, similar to Silicon Valley but in Alabama. The people he was working with there had bought a building. Tom, Kyle, and some other people, you can probably look this up, but they were helping to work on the Cyber-Party and they were instrumental to some of the initial videos for the Cyber Party. We quickly figured out that it was super expensive to create a political party, and so John decided to run under the libertarian banner, or maybe he was approached by someone and asked if he wanted to be there. I'm not sure how that came about that, but he was then running for president under the libertarian banner.

There were a lot of things happening around our home by this point, we moved to our second home on Beasley Drive. It was a bigger home, more land, and a nicer neighbourhood, but still in Lexington, and we were a little closer to our head of security who was now only five minutes away. At that time, we had three dogs: Marley the big white dog, Tequila, and Coco who was a black and brown mutt, so we were adding more dogs to our family.

Now, at the time of the shooting, I'm not sure exactly what was going on. It could have been the fact that I hadn't told John about the pimp and what was going on, and so he was concerned. In that house, we had a huge attic space next to the bedrooms that were up on the top floor. Anybody could have hidden there. We also had a massive crawlspace underneath the house, so John was concerned that people could get in there and hide in that crawlspace or the attic space. He eventually put blocks on the entrances to block it off, as he was concerned that people could easily get in there. I think John's concern was also that maybe I was assisting them.

I'm not sure if there was anyone in the house, I certainly wasn't any part of putting anyone in the house, but because I hadn't spoken to John about what I did know, he suspected me of being part of it. Other people worked for us at the time who he also suspected of being nefarious, in what way I wasn't entirely sure, but he was very suspicious of one particular person.

As for the shooting, I don't even know how to tell that story. John felt uncomfortable one night and he thought he could hear movement in the crawlspace. I couldn't hear anything, but I didn't know what to listen for. This particular night he just randomly started firing shots, but this wasn't the only house he did this in; he did this in previous houses. He did the same at 'The Tree House' as well, but there was someone there on that occasion.

At that previous house, he saw a shadow of someone standing out under the carport, which was right outside of our bedroom window, so he fired through the wall with his shotgun, not intending to shoot the person but just to scare them off, and it worked, and we saw the camera footage.

The shooting in Tennessee was something that he allowed to be in the newspapers, he wanted that information out there for whatever reason, but to explain that time, he was just uncomfortable. He told me to sit on my hands and not move, so that's what I did, he was very serious and then he started yelling at whomever he thought may be out there, and he would just fire randomly.

I never went under the crawl space but he did have his security go under there with him and they found that the ground was disturbed where people had previously been, so there was a legitimate concern knowing people had been in there. The same was true of the attic space, there were a couple of soda cans and wrappers found, so this was not just some random crazy thing he was doing with absolutely no reason or no purpose, there was evidence that people had been around. That's the explanation for the shooting.

WHACKD – Do you have any stories of potential assassination attempts on John's life or times you both felt in danger?

Janice McAfee – Oh, there were lots of those. Okay, so let's start from the beginning. When John was doing his talks there were always constant threats, even just simply people trying to get him drinks. I remember one specific incident, John was talking and in the middle of speaking this person went: "Here John, I got you this drink," he brought so much attention to himself but John took it and he would either put it down in a way as to not to alert the other person or his head of security John Pool would discreetly deal with it. In this specific incident, I took the drink myself and brought a new one to him. I remember him taking a sip out of it and then looking at it and I said "It's okay, I got that drink for you, you can trust me." I wasn't gonna hurt him.

I think my attempts to warn him about the things that I was being asked to do, with the spare keys to the flat, or the poison in the food — and because I didn't do those things, and I instead warned him about it — built some trust. He could feel safe knowing that I wouldn't let anything happen to him if it was within my power. It took a lot to build that trust, it was still something that carried on throughout our relationship whenever I would bring him a drink, I would still take a sip of it and let him see me do that, but just to let him know it's cool. It's not that I had to, or that he asked me to, it was just something I did naturally just to reassure him. Later into our relationship, he started to let me cook for him, so slowly some trust was built over time.

So, to these dangerous situations. The first thing happened in Portland, by the time the Belizean soccer team came to play in the summer of 2013. Not all of them left, and John shared this information. It was in the summer of 2013, maybe July, the Belizean soccer team came to play soccer in Portland, Oregon. Of all the places for them to play, it's where we are. From what John told me, they were shit in the tournament, whatever the tournament was. I remember reading a sports article saying that they weren't good at all and that whomever they played against found they were no competition, and that they were shocked at how bad they were. John also said they had never come to America to play, and the fact that they came to Portland, Oregon, where we were living, was no coincidence.

Our address had also been exposed after John did some interviews and they published our address in the story, the name of the apartment we were staying in as well as the crosswalk, with pictures, so people knew exactly where we were living. After the soccer team supposedly came and left, people who didn't live there started showing up in our neighbourhood. We were very familiar with our neighbours. We started seeing these Caribbean-looking people showing up in the neighbourhood. Our apartment had a 180-degree view of the road watching all the traffic, and people who seemed to be casing the building. It was September of that year when the first major attempt on John happened, in that apartment building.

By then John had hired this guy named Rocky. He was part of a biker gang in Portland, he was able to carry guns and we needed some security presence. He was a tough guy. John's head of security John Pool was still living in Tennessee, so we needed someone here with us physically. So, Rocky began driving us around whenever we went out, even if we were just going out on a date, he would always be around somewhere with us. Then his girlfriend came on as well because she was also part of the biker gang and these people could legally carry guns, so that was very important.

IN MEMORIAM: MCAFEE REMEMBERED

So, in September of that year, there was an article that came out about John, and it said that he had died of an overdose in a casino in Las Vegas. If you look for it you might still find that article, this was when he tweeted out that "the news of my death is grossly exaggerated" or something to that effect. When the story came out, he was getting phone calls all day from people asking Are you dead? People were concerned about him, so he put out the tweet. A couple of days later Rocky was arrested on trumped-up charges, so we didn't have our security, and we were home alone. We weren't afraid to be alone, but it helped to have security around, especially someone who could not only carry weapons but also who knew how to use them.

So, the same week after our security was arrested, there was a night when John and I were up just binge-watching Family Guy. Our apartment was an L shape and facing the main road was our bedroom window, where we could go position ourselves in various places to get a full view of what was happening down below on the street. So, we're watching television in our bedroom and I happen to look out the window. I see this construction truck pull up to the stoplight on the main road, and that catches my attention, so I'm kind of tuning out of the show now and I'm now more focused on what was happening down on the street. This is what we did, keep an eye on the surroundings.

So, this man gets out of the truck and he's wearing that fluorescent work dress and he walks over to one of the streetlights and he's kind of just messing with it, but not doing anything. Then while he's standing there, he faces down Hawthorn to the side street and flashes his flashlight four times, so I told John and he looks, then the man flashes his torch again and immediately John's like "Okay, turn off the lights, turn off the TV." So, everything was completely dark now.

John takes up a position in the living room, he could see the truck that was parked in the street and we could see down the smaller side streets. He said he could hear a car idling. I couldn't hear what he was listening for but I was getting tired now. About an hour or so later, I'm really tired and I can't stay up any longer, so I went and I lay down to go to sleep.

Then, it's about two in the morning and John comes running into the bedroom to wake me up, saying "Get up, they're here, we've got to leave now, they're here," and I'm like "What, who's here, what's going on, it's the middle of the night, this is crazy." John's like "Listen, that's fine, if you don't want to come that's fine, you will be safe, they won't bother you, but I have to leave."

So, I was like "Okay, well wait for a second." I threw something on quickly and I asked if I should bring a gun, but he said "No, it might be the cops, so don't." He said he saw two motorcycles, a sedan and a garbage truck, and it was the truck he said he had heard idling. So, we ran out, left our apartment and ran down the opposite end of the hallway down into the parking garage below.

So, we're in this parking garage and the lights are triggered by motion detection, so the lights are on, and John's running around frantically looking for somewhere to hide. Our building was situated on top of a dental office and a small café, so there were multiple ways to get into the restaurant or the dental office from the parking garage, there were also storage units there. So, there were lots of little doors, and John's trying to see if any of them were unlocked, but they weren't.

I'm thinking "What the fuck is going on?" then I hear something idling outside of the garage and John's running around like crazy looking for somewhere to hide, and I'm looking at the cameras thinking "Oh my God when they see this footage, they're gonna think we are batshit crazy running around here at the middle of the night." Then John goes into the trash room where this big trash bin is and he's like "Get in, you have to hide in here." I'm like "Fuck that, that's nasty." I was wearing a dress so I'm thinking about all the nasty stuff in there, like "No, I'm not getting in there." So, he closes the trash bin and then he turns the light off in there and closes the door.

He's looking around now and he sees this car elevator system. It moved around like an elevator: there was a lower level, the main level and then a top level. If your car was on the top, you would press one of the buttons and it would rotate down to where you could get in your car. So, John looks up to the second level and he's like "Can you climb up there?" he climbs up first and he gets under one of the cars and then I climb up next to him. I was wearing a dress and it was hanging down behind the back by the wall, luckily, I had the presence of mind to pull that up, just in case something was happening. I didn't want to give away our hiding place by letting my dress be seen, so I pulled it up under the car to make sure we were gonna be safe, and finally, the motion detection lights turn off.

To get into the garage and building there's a key card that you put up against the lock and it unlocks with a very loud click, and so the lights are off for about five minutes then we hear the click, the lights come on, and they stay on.

We could hear movement, but not enough to make out footsteps. We couldn't hear the stepping or walking, but we could feel it as the motion passed, moving around the parking garage, whoever it was. I'm not sure if it was one person or more than one. I did attempt to look, but I couldn't see anyone from where we were positioned. In the meantime, in the main lobby, we can hear people running up the stairways. It was pretty loud. Then, it was about four in the morning when they opened up the gate of the parking garage and they rolled out that large trash bin.

They had found out that we weren't in our apartment, so now they were trying to find out where we were in the building because there was ultimately only one main exit, so they would have seen us coming if we left. So, the assumption was that we had to still be somewhere in the building and so the fact that John turned the light off in the trash room made them believe that we were in the trash bin. They rolled the trash bin out to the garbage truck, dumped it, compressed the garbage and then rolled the trash bin back into the trash room. A half-hour later in the lobby, we heard someone yell "FUCK" really, really loud, like they'd realised that we weren't in the trash bin because we weren't in the back of the garbage truck. By this time, it was getting late, they couldn't stay much longer because people would start getting up to go to work soon. They were trying to do all of this under the cover of night, and we could be anywhere by now, so they had also lost the advantage.

All they had to do, whoever was in that parking garage looking for us, all they had to do was bend over and look underneath the cars on that elevator and they would eventually have found us, underneath the car on that second level. That's all they had to do. I was scared shitless. I was so nervous and scared under there and then John starts to fall asleep and I nudge him like "What the fuck are you doing, wake up." He was napping like "It's cool, be cool." We couldn't talk, but he was trying to reassure me and I was freaking out, but I wasn't making noise or bringing attention to myself.

After they realised that we weren't there, they eventually left. It was about seven in the morning and then the apartment manager arrived. Something I should also add, when we initially moved into the apartment, the apartment manager was a woman called Virginia, and she was very nice. Our dog Tequila had snuck out of our apartment a few times. I don't know how she got out, she's very smart and she figured out how to open the door. So, she would be in the hallway just running around greeting people. Fortunately, she was a very nice dog, even though she was a Pitbull. Virginia would have to call us and tell us our dog was in the hallway, so we were very familiar with our manager. Then suddenly there was a post on our door, on everybody's doors, just alerting the people in the building that the building had been sold that August and they were going to have new management immediately coming in, and the next week, she's gone.

This new manager took her place, a man, and he wasn't doing anything that we were familiar with Virginia doing. It was an apartment building, his job was to answer questions or solve any issues that were happening in the building and he wouldn't do that, so already this person was very suspicious and John was very suspicious of him. John later found out who bought the building, but that's a whole other story, which also has connections to Belize.

So, this apartment manager comes in at about seven in the morning, he goes directly into the room where the security cameras are and where they have the recording devices, he stays in there for a couple of minutes and then he walks out. We assume that he went in there to get the security footage because obviously, everything that had happened would be on the security cameras.

We stayed there on the car elevator for about another hour. We didn't come out until like 9 am when people started to get up and get into their cars. So, we get up from under there and we immediately call Rocky's girlfriend and tell her what happened and we ask her if she could come with us because we're going to be leaving town. She was able to come. So, we're packing. John said, "Pack what you can, and let's go."

So, when we get back to our apartment, our dog would normally come to greet us at the door, every time she'd be right there wagging her tail happily greeting us, so we are calling out to her from the front door before we even walked in because we weren't sure if anyone was in there or not. So, we're calling her and she didn't come, which was very, very strange. When we go in, she's sitting on her bed, not wagging her tail or anything. She's just sitting on the bed, which was super strange behaviour. So, something had happened, even to her. What that was I do not know, she didn't have any bruises or anything, but something happened to her that traumatised her to the point where she wouldn't get up.

So, we packed our things. Just as we were leaving, we happen to see one of our neighbours, whom we'd seen before on different occasions and whom we were friendly with, she was an older woman. We were chatting with her whilst waiting for the elevator to come John asked her: "Did you hear anything strange happen last night?" And she said, "Yes, I did, I was just going down to ask the manager if something was happening because I heard all of this noise in the hallway of people running up and down the hallway, there was a lot of talking going on in the middle of the night." That confirmed for us what we already knew.

Once we get down to the lobby she goes off and speaks to the manager. We're taking our time as we eavesdrop on the conversation to hear what he says to her. He says "Oh no, there was nothing, you know, no incidents." She was asking if there was some sort of medical emergency or something and he's just like "No, nothing out of the ordinary." Immediately I'm thinking 'Okay, that sounds crazy.' At the very least I thought he would have mentioned us running around looking stupid in the parking garage or something, but he never mentioned it.

He had his back to us and then John comes around into his view saying something to the effect of "Yeah, we heard all this crazy commotion," and then all the blood drained from the man's face, he looks at us like "What the fuck are you guys doing here?" He looked super scared, and that told us everything that we needed to know about his possible involvement.

Once we were then settled in Colorado, we had Rocky pack up our things in the apartment there in Portland for them to be shipped to us in Colorado. John had this back-and-forth conversation with that same apartment manager, saying "Listen, I know who you are, I know what happened, I know who bought the building and I know their connection to the Cartel and Belize, and I'm giving all this information to the FBI." He then told them he had hidden cameras all over that building, even cameras in the elevator. Then when Rocky went there to the apartment building to pack our stuff he went to the elevator, and they had all of the panels down. They had stripped the elevator of all the panels trying to find cameras that weren't there, that was another confirmation that they were part of whatever went down there.

The next thing that happened as far as danger would have been in Colorado, in 2014. John had been doing interviews all along at this point and he had an interview with CNN, I believe it was. So, we go there to the studio in Colorado and John asks the reporter "Please do not put my location as part of your story." But for whatever reason, the reporter immediately reports "From Colorado Springs, it's John McAfee." So, now people knew where we were.

Just like what happened in Portland after the Belizean soccer team, people started showing up in Colorado Springs. It isn't that big of a town but people started turning up in our neighbourhood, so John put cameras all around the property and he had bars installed on the windows. We lived in a double-wide trailer and I adored that house, it was always one of my favourite houses. My second favourite was the house we had on Hatteras Island in North Carolina. It was just a cosy house and it was awesome. It had spare bedrooms and John let me decorate them for my kids for whenever they might visit so we would be comfortable. He taught me how to make a fire too, we were always making fires in the fireplace. It was awesome.

After our location was reported we were doing all of these things to get our security beefed up and one time that John was going out of town he wanted me to stay at a hotel, just to be out of the house and away from the neighbourhood. As I said, there were suspicious people in our area.

So, I was staying at this hotel with our dog Tequila and I had to take her to the bathroom, so I took her for a walk outside. It was snowing at the time, there was lots of snow on the ground and Tequila was running around all happy in the snowfall. Then this car pulled up into the parking lot from the main road and parked there, they were just watching me. There was a man and a woman in the car and the woman got her phone out with its camera facing me taking my picture or recording me.

I watched them but I didn't go too close. I was very concerned. As soon as Tequila was finished, I went inside and told John what happened. He said: "Be careful, don't go outside if you don't need to, stay indoors." So that's what I did, and then he came back.

Before we decided to leave that place, we went to the FBI and John told them, who he was, what happened in Belize, why he thinks people are after him, and what happened in Portland. He informs them of all these things, he tells them about the pimp, the cartel, and that we've been threatened by all of these things. I wasn't in the room with him the entire time, but I'm sure he explained everything to the agent. Then the FBI wanted to question me which was strange. Why would they want to question me? I remember we did go into their office and there was a brief talking where John gave an overview of why he thought people were after him and then I was asked to leave, so it was just John in there. He told me later on that that he shared all the details with them, but they never actually questioned me. They just said they would look into it, but they never did. Nothing ever came of it. John informed the agent about what had happened with people in our neighbourhood, but nobody came out to do anything.

We decided at that point to leave and go to Tennessee to stay with John's Head of Security because we would be safe there. Nobody knew where he lived and he lived out in the country, if anything happened there, we could properly defend ourselves with no problem. So, we went there.

Lots of little things like that happened once we moved into our homes in Tennessee. We had three different homes in that state. We had one on Circle Drive 'The Tree House,' one on Beasley Drive, and we had another one on Lakeshore Drive, which was the last house we lived there in Tennessee. John had cameras in every place, but people being in the crawlspace or attic spaces was always a concern, no matter who lived with us, or where we lived.

In the last place we lived, there were a lot more people living with us and it was where 'Team McAfee' was created. At that point, John had live-in security. Jimmy Watson was one but there were a lot of other ex-military people there. Josh and Andrew were others, and then there was Luke Jenkins, who wasn't security, but he was a part of Team McAfee.

In that last place something John found someone in the crawlspace. You could see where they had urinated after John had been shooting under there, so that was very intense. But there were a lot of these things happening, but nothing like what happened in Portland until we get to North Carolina.

Before we get to that, there was an incident where I was almost kidnapped. It was a kidnapping attempt on me in 2014 when we were in Boston. We were in Boston meeting a director that XXXXXXXX has found and wants to introduce us to, his name is XXXXX. He's the director of XXXXXXX XXXXXX, which was his documentary. So XXXXXXXX is there in Boston, introducing this person, and we meet the director.

At the time John and I were fighting and it was bad. I'm not sure exactly what we were fighting about, but it came down to the fact that I was still refusing to come clean to him about my pimp. There had been plenty of opportunities for me to do so at this point, and I wanted to, but I just didn't trust it. So, he's like "I don't want to be with you anymore," so I leave the hotel to get some air.

As I leave the hotel, to the left, I see someone standing smoking so I ask if they know a place nearby to get some cigarettes. They tell me if I go through the parking garage, there's a store right there. Normally, I wouldn't go down in those kinds of parking garages, they aren't safe places at night, especially for women. But I figured it was safe so I quickly walk through. I see a car parked outside the parking garage and there was a white man just sitting there in his car, smoking a cigarette.

Immediately my attention is drawn to that, but I go across to the store and I buy a pack of cigarettes and a can of Red Bull. After I come out of the store, I sit on one of the benches by the bus stop and smoke two cigarettes just watching the traffic, the people and I also watch the person who is still parked, not on the phone, or reading, but just parked there, still smoking cigarettes. I figure it was safe enough for me to walk back to the hotel, but because I saw this guy parked sitting outside it, I wasn't going to go back through the parking garage because someone could have easily pulled up and snatched me, it's that easy.

So, I didn't do that, I decided to walk around the block to get back to the hotel and as I'm walking down the street, I see this woman coming from the opposite direction walking towards me. She doesn't look suspicious, but something that I learned from John was to just randomly stop walking, he would do this sometimes. Just stop, and watch what happens around you. So, sure enough, I stopped just to see what she would do. I turned to look at the woman to see how she was going to react and she seems confused about what to do next, then she randomly changes direction and walks over to a building to look at the window as though there was something she was interested in. Me being an asshole, I'm like "I see you, ma'am, you've been spotted, you can go ahead and leave now," and so she continued back down the road.

I made it to the intersection and I let the light sequence roll through a full cycle before I decide to cross the street watching for any movements of people or cars. I finally walk down the street; I just have to make a square back to where my hotel is. Then I get to the next main intersection, and the next one, and I stand there to watch the cars and the foot traffic, right before the light turns red, I then decide to cross the street, I wanted to wait to be sure that no one was in the crosswalk.

So, I feel relatively safe that no one was around following me and immediately as I'm crossing the street, I don't know where the fuck they came from, but these three men were behind me immediately. They're black men, but they're not American, they looked Caribbean. I'm walking, paying attention to it and now I'm looking up ahead of me. What am I walking into? Are there more people behind me?

So, there's an office building next to the parking garage on the corner, there's a little cubby on the side of the building where people can sit and a Mexican man is sitting there, he has tattoos on his face and he's sitting directly across from this old yellow panel van. Immediately I notice that, and I'm like "Okay, fuck, if I keep walking, are they going to snatch me and throw me in the truck?" They're pretty close to me by now, these three men behind me, and I'm within arm's reach. Before I get close enough to the van doors I immediately dart in the gap between the back of the van and the car that was right behind it, into the middle of the street and across the street. I didn't look for traffic I just ran across over towards the hospital before they could do anything. I was so fucking scared. I sat at the hospital just to watch. I don't know what happened to those three men, I don't know where they went, thankfully they never moved at me, but I didn't see where they might have gone to.

I immediately got back to the hotel and told John what happened. He then informed me that he received a tweet from Wendy. She worked with us while we were in Tennessee and she was also with us when we were living at the Tree House. She had sent him a screenshot of a tweet that said "John McAfee" and it gave the name of a cell phone store and the city. Now that cell phone store was the store that we had visited only a few days earlier to purchase brand new cell phones, and instead of using cash John used his bank card. But now we had another confirmation that someone was reporting our whereabouts publicly on Twitter.

John was immediately like "No, we're leaving," and XXXXXXXX was trying to say "Are you sure, nothing's happening," and John's like "No, I trust Janice, she knows what she's talking about, if someone tried to kidnap her, we are leaving, she wouldn't lie about that." So, XXXXXXXX was just trying to dissuade us from leaving.

IN MEMORIAM: MCAFEE REMEMBERED

We got a ride to the airport and we took nothing with us but the clothes on our backs, and the necessary ID that we needed, but no electronics. We left it all there and went to London.

John didn't feel safe staying in London because we went to the airport with XXXXXXXX and the director, so they knew where we were flying to and which hotel we were staying in. This is why we didn't stay there but ended up going to Scotland.

On the plane to England, John got talking to this man and for whatever reason, he tells the man his story and what's happening, about how we're hiding out and all that stuff, then this man invites us to his home. I wasn't able to thank him properly and I'm not sure if John ever was able to properly thank him, but it would be nice if he can read this.

Before touching down on that flight John already wanted to get on the next flight out of England, which happened to be to Scotland, so that's also why we ended up needing to go there. So, this man invited us to stay with him, which was sweet, as his wife was out of town. John was like "Are you sure it's okay for us to stay?" And he was like "Yeah."

The day that we were there he took us to someplace to eat that he liked, we paid for the food and the taxi as John was taking care of the expenses, but he was such a nice man. When his wife came home, she was like, "Who the fuck are these people?" She didn't say that, but her face said it all. I think she was super pissed off, not happy at all, but she tried to be gracious. I said, "John, we have to leave." He's like "Yeah, I know, poor guy." We felt really bad because we knew he was gonna catch a tonne of shit from his wife when we left.

The next day we went and stayed at a hotel in Scotland which was close to Trump's Golf Resort. It was a very nice area and it was there that I came clean to John about everything, so there's that.

Okay, so the next big thing that happened, let's see. After the situation in Portland, we went to Colorado, because John had friends there. This is after our location was reported on the news, the fact that we were in Colorado Springs. So, at that point, we were staying in various hotels throughout the area.

This one time we were staying at a hotel close to the airport because I was going to be leaving soon to catch a flight to see my kids in California. I went routinely around their birthdays and the school holidays. This was my routine of how often I went to see the kids. When they weren't in school, I was there visiting. John would often go with me to see them, which was nice, but this time he wasn't going with me.

Before I leave the hotel to go to the airport there seem to be strange movements happening around the hotel. The hotel was on a strip, just dozens of hotels with a street that runs along behind them to the main road. We happened to be outside and there was this truck. It would drive to one hotel, sit there for a few minutes, then drive to the next hotel, sit there, and so on. What John deduced from that behaviour was that they had a Stingray and that they were trying to pinpoint what hotel we were in. As John is watching I say to him "Are you sure you don't want to come with me to California? Whatever's happening here, at least you could get away from that too," and he's like "No, I'm gonna stay here."

So, I leave. I'm there in California and I get this call from John, he's like "I'm hiding out in the parking garage, there are people here at the hotel." I'm like "Oh shit, do you want me to come to you? What can I do?" and he's like "No, just stay there with the kids. I'll figure this out. I'll get out of here." I don't know what transpired in that timeframe but he said he would call me when he could. I was freaking out and worried about him. Eventually, he calls me saying that he's driven up to me in California, so I ended up cutting my trip short by a few days because John said it wasn't safe there. He said he had been followed since Denver and at various stops. He was able to lose the pursuers. We didn't figure out until later how people were following us: it was the LoJack in John's truck.

We always had brand-new phones and we weren't using any of the phones that we had previously used. I would only call my family, my sister or my parents to talk to my kids, but then that was it. I would take the battery out of my phone — this was when you could still remove batteries from the phone — to be sure that your phone was actually off. So, I didn't have to worry about that on my end, and John knew what he was doing as far as keeping us secure. So, we ended up leaving and just driving, we didn't have a destination in mind but we were trying to figure out how these people were still on us, and how they were tailing us, because now they were tailing us.

It wasn't a few hours behind or a few days. They were tailing us everywhere that we went. You could see the cars following. Multiple cars were on our tail, so we were just trying to shake these people and so eventually we made our way to Flagstaff in Arizona. Before we arrived, we were on the highway in Arizona and John spotted a jeep off to the side of the road, it was just kinda tucked in the brush. In Arizona, there's a lot of desert area, a lot of empty lands where there's nothing but dirt and brush. But I saw the Jeep as well, and I don't know why but it drew our attention. Then there was a strange sound that happened. I don't even know how to explain it, but it just sounded fucking weird. The radio wasn't on, and this alien noise went by, and I later found out John believed that it was a bullet ricocheting off the 18-Wheeler right as we were getting ready to pass it in the other lane. John gave an interview talking about this, he never said it to me, but I always was like "What the fuck was that noise?" I don't know what that was, but I do know that there were lots of people following us. Maybe they were trying to disable our truck, I don't know.

Then, when we arrived in Flagstaff and called Rocky's girlfriend who had rented a car, to meet us there. We gave her our location and had our Head of Security with us, John Pool. So, she and John Pool rode together in the rental car.

Later, we were all at this Walmart and as usual cars were pulling in, and we are all on edge. We recognised one or two of the suspicious cars that we had seen following before, and so we point them out to our Head of Security, John Pool. He then figured out we were being tracked by the LoJack in John's truck, so then John and I got into the rental car, and we left John Pool with John's truck.

Around the time of the attempt on us at our apartment building in Portland, John and I were talking about safety measures. I said, "John, what if we have to go on the run or something, I can put a wig on, but I will still look like me." Then he suggested "You know, you're right. You could get a burka?" So, I go online and I'm shopping for burkas. Initially, I only bought the Hijab, the veil that covers my face but then I saw they sold the full Burka, where all you could see was the eyes, so I bought that. I had the Burka with me while we were travelling. I kept it with us when we were still living in hotels. At the time, we hadn't bought our place in Colorado yet.

So, I get in this rental car with this burka on. It's Arizona and it's hot, we're about an hour's drive out from where we left our truck, so I'm still on edge. Rocky's girlfriend is driving, John's in the passenger seat and I'm in the backseat. I'm watching vehicles, making sure nobody's following, but I'm freaking out. John's trying to calm me down, you know: "We're fine, it's just adrenaline, everything's fine." Somehow, she turns off the main road and we end up on this fucking dirt road, I don't even know how, all we had to do was stay somewhere that was populated, and somehow, we're on this dirt road.

We end up with this canyon rock to the right of us and a sheer drop on the left and we're on this one-lane road. I don't know how the fuck we ended up there, but finally, we get through that, but then there's this car about a mile or two behind us as we get back to a main road out of the canyon and I said to John "Listen, I will calm down if you drive, John. I will be calm." I knew if something was happening, and if danger arose significantly, we would be okay with John driving.

So now John's driving, we're back in the populated town area. We were running low on gas and we are at this stoplight with a gas station on the left. I said "John, you might want to get some gas now" and he was like "No, I think we'll be fine." Then I notice something and say "If that white truck that you see right there turns here and follows us when we turn, I want you to know we are being followed." We turned the corner, and sure as shit, the truck is now behind us.

John slows down, like right down, and then the other car does the same, it's a two-lane zone, and then John speeds up, more, and more, and more, and he continued to speed up until we finally got up to 124 mph. I remember looking at the speedometer. Rocky's girlfriend is freaked out, yelling at John to slow down, because we're coming up on other cars that fast, it's fucking spooky coming up on cars like that.

The pursuing truck is behind us the whole time, the entire time chasing us. I was glad I asked John to drive. Fuck, if we hit something or lost control, we would have rolled for like a mile. We were in a little Ford Focus, and John often said if Ford Focus wanted to, he could do them an awesome sales commercial for their Ford Focus. It was a little Ford Focus hatchback rental car, and John got that little sucker all the way up to 124 mph.

Eventually, after about 10 minutes of this, they slowed down, it was probably even freakier for them as they were in a much larger vehicle going that fast. We were able to manoeuvre quickly around cars in our lane at speed, whereas they had to slow down to overtake, so they eventually slowed down but John maintained that 124 mph until we got into the next town.

We went deep enough in so that we had enough lead time to get gas and then get back on the road. At the gas station, I put my burka back on, we got our gas, and then we got on the highway out of town.

WHACKD – John posted on Twitter in 2018 that he had been poisoned with the tweet 'A message to my incompetent enemies' from a hospital bed. Can you describe a little about that event?

Janice McAfee – In North Carolina, before we purchased our house, we went and spent some time there, to see if we wanted to live there, and so we were staying at this vacation home. John had his live-in security with us and their significant other, and I think we just celebrated the Fourth of July or something. Some other people came into town, and I was getting ready to leave for the summer vacation to see my kids for a couple of weeks, and the mood had shifted in the home. That's the only way I can explain it, but I was concerned.

Nothing particularly stood out, nothing happened that caused me to be concerned, but there was just a change in the energy. Jimmy was taking his wife to the airport, she was going out of town, and I was going to ride with them to the airport. I told John "I don't know what it is, but something seems off. Just be careful. If you want me to stay, I can go late," and he was like "No, just go. It's okay, you can go,

I'll be fine." I was like "Are you sure?" And he said something to me which I never forgot, he said "Remember me when I'm gone."

I think he knew something was afoot, but he just didn't tell me. But I leave and arrive in California, then I call him and we talked, like "Everything's cool." He had people visiting him, but Jimmy, his security, wasn't there. He trusted Jimmy more than the other security, but he was about an hour or so drive away with his wife from where we lived, on Hatteras Island in North Carolina.

A day or two later I get a call from Jimmy. He says "Ms Janice, don't freak out, but John is in the hospital. We had an ambulance come to get him and he's in the hospital on a ventilator." This is fucking bad.

Even worse, I couldn't leave California yet as I had a court case to get visitation for my kids so I would able to visit with them without a family member present. Even though they were living with my parents there was a situation where I had to go through the courts to be able to visit them without the supervision of a family member. I was able to have my sister visit with me if the kids were to be with me alone, you know, separate from being at my parents' house. So, I had to go to court for that, and I couldn't reschedule it.

Jimmy would call me every day. He would put the phone to John's ear and I would talk to him, just telling him I love him and how I would be coming to his side as soon as I could, as soon as the court case was over that Thursday. My flight was already booked.

I couldn't tell my family because I didn't want anybody to know that John was in the hospital. It's very dangerous to be in the hospital; he would have been very vulnerable. Enough mob movies have attested to the fact that if you want to do someone harm, it's easier to get to them when they are in a hospital or prison.

So, I made it to the hospital and immediately Jimmy and XXXXXXXX came out to meet us. I won't speak publicly about this person, but I think this person had a lot to do with what happened at the hospital.

Jimmy gave me an update. He said, "The boss is pissed off because they won't take him off the ventilator." They had him on a ventilator, so he was writing these angry notes saying 'You don't know who the fuck I am' and 'Google me.'

Then XXXXXXXX was telling me: "Listen, John's going to want you to take him off the ventilator, but you can't do that because it's dangerous. He could die if that happens." He's trying to scare me, he's like: "We will just see how John is first and decide then." He was pushing me into this. "Don't let him off the ventilator."

When we get to John's room in the hospital, I brace myself. My brother had just recently died so I was expecting to see John in a similar condition to how my brother was. I didn't know what to expect with him being on a ventilator because that means he was in bad shape, right?

So, I get in there and he doesn't at all look like someone that needs to be on a ventilator. He's sitting up with a notepad in his hand and when he sees me, he breaks down and we hug, he almost squeezed me to death. He squeezed me so tight and I was crying, he was so happy to see me.

I asked him what had been going on just trying to get a beat on the situation and then the doctor comes in, he's giving me that same energy that XXXXXXXX was with us, you know: "Oh he is very, very ill and he needs to stay on this ventilator, if you take him off this ventilator, he may die."

The doctors were trying to get me to understand, or trying to scare me into a decision by basically saying if I take him off the ventilator, I will kill him. We were still married at the time so I had to make that medical decision for him, so that's why they were focused on me in this way. They were saying his oxygen levels are low and so the machine is breathing for him, they point out some numbers on the machine telling me they were low and this is why he needs to remain on it.

At the time John has this notepad so he begins writing this note, it said something to the effect of: 'My name is John McAfee, I do not wish to be on this ventilator any longer, I demand that you take it off immediately,' followed by the date to attest to the fact that he's of sound mind. He was saying "Take me off this fucking ventilator now because I don't want it anymore."

There were two nurses and the doctor in the room and they were going back and forth arguing with John so I said "Just hold up, stop. We all stood there and witnessed him write this note, did we not? He wrote this note on his own by his hand, did he not? So clearly, he's of sound mind and body, he knows what he's asking for, he understands the risk, and he's clearly expressed what his wishes are, so take him off the ventilator. There's no need to go back and forth on this, just do it already." The doctor then said "Fine." He told the nurse to start making the preparations and then they take the tube out of his throat, that's what a ventilator is, so they take it out.

I go to hug him again, and in my ear, John whispers "They were going to try to kill me, they were going to put something in the ventilator to kill me." That's what he told me, and that XXXXXX tried to poison him. So, this same person I'm not naming is also in our company. John tells me this in my ear but I don't react to it, obviously, with that person being in the room. So, we continue as normal, but he shared this with me.

Then I asked the nurse to show me his oxygen levels now he was off the ventilator. I said "What are his oxygen levels? Show me what number that is on the machine." It was at the same number as when he was on the ventilator. His oxygen levels were normal, but for whatever reason, the doctor was telling me that this other lower number was his oxygen levels. The nurse pointed to something else saying that was his oxygen level and just by remembering what the screens looked like the first time, I noticed the doctor pointed to something completely different the second time around. It was weird.

Everyone had been there with John for days, they hadn't left, so when I got there Ty was working security to relieve Jimmy so that he could shower, rest and everything else. When XXXXXXXX was also gone long enough so that it was just John and me, we were able to talk privately.

He told me what happened to him the day that he ended up in the hospital, He said he went out on the boat, he took XXXXXXXX and whatever security he would have had with him and they were talking about drinking. When they got back to the vacation home that we were renting at the time, this same person had made him a drink. John told me that the last thing he remembers was XXXXXXXX bringing him the drink, and then drinking it, and that's it.

WHACKD – So you're in California, Jimmy isn't with John, and John drinks this drink at home with XXXXXXXX, what happens from there?

Janice McAfee – As Jimmy explained it to me that when he finally got back to our home from being with his wife, he said the house was completely dark and quiet. He said he was called out to see where everyone was, but nobody was answering. He finally finds somebody and they say John had gone to bed, so he trusted that. Eventually for whatever reason Jimmy wanted to go and check on John but when he approached the bedroom John didn't answer. He went into the room and found John on the floor gasping for air, his whole body was red and he had been vomiting.

So that's how we found him, they call the ambulance and that's how he got to the hospital. So, that was a major situation. There was also a puncture wound on his foot that he showed me, I had taken a picture of it and it looked like he had been injected, that is what it looked like, a little injection spot. Nothing showed up in any toxicology report other than marijuana, but there are many drugs that you can put in someone and it not be traceable. So, those were some of the major things that happened.

WHACKD – Just after that point you both get your home in North Carolina. Can you share any memorable stories from that time?

Janice McAfee – North Carolina was fucking awesome. We bought a house there. 'The Love Boat,' was the name of it. It was shaped like a boat and it was a cool house, it was just so peaceful and so beautiful. I loved being by the water too, there is something very healing for me about being near the water. I would take the dogs to the beach and it was just nice. We lived in the south and it was a quiet area of water to be on.

We had a little guest house right on the bank of the water so we would walk down there from the main property with the dogs and they would do their thing, run around, pee on things, and have fun. It was just a big adventure for them and it was a really good place.

Now, some other memorable things happened. Well, there was a breakdown in the relationship between John and Josh, who was one of John's security staff. John had to let him go because we found money missing from bank accounts that he had control over. There were a lot of other nefarious activities that later John became aware of, and later told me about surrounding 'Team McAfee.' This was when a huge amount of funds had gone missing and that was also one of the reasons why we left Tennessee; that whole relationship had broken down. One important thing to note is that John didn't have any properties or cars in his name, the houses were always in my name, John intended for them to be for me. He got somewhere that would be big enough for the kids to visit as that was something he always wanted to ensure I had. He was always concerned about making sure that I would be okay, even if we parted ways. He wanted to know I would never be in a situation where I feel I have to go back to the life that he found me in. He was very worried about that, so allowing me to have the houses in my name was his way to make me feel secure. So, the houses were in my name but the cars were in the names of the various security staff, with Josh being one of them.

Josh had some of these cars in his name and we didn't know that he was sending people to repo the vehicle. John could sense that something was happening, but he just didn't know what at the time. He had been up for a couple of days at this point and when it got dark, he would have everyone turn the lights off. We could watch TV but it had to be quiet, and he would go from the living room to our bedroom, watching and listening, watching the cameras, flashing the flashlights, checking places and doing all this stuff. So, everybody's on edge and getting tired and sick of it, so I had to say "Listen, nine times out of ten, it's nothing happening, but that one time it is, you're gonna be glad that he's like this."

That night, the dogs are barking at something. We had a balcony from our bedroom and the balcony was overlooking the pool, car park, and the street below. The dogs were barking at something. John goes out and thinks he can see something, so he fires a shot, not to hurt anybody, and not to hit anything, but just a warning shot to scare people, and it did scare people. Sure as shit, early that next morning, these guys come to the property. Jimmy goes down to meet them, like "Who the fuck are you?" They're on high alert, like "What the fuck are you doing here?" And the men that arrived are like "We're repo men, here to repossess one of these vehicles." The vehicle was in Josh's name, but Jimmy didn't let them do that, so they were sent on their way.

I said to everybody "See, John knew." He sensed it. We didn't know what was happening, but John did, and so I said "Whenever he gets in one of those moods again, just let him do what he needs to do to feel comfortable." By this point, I had learned that.

Early on, I would tell him "Nothing is happening, we can calm down," but that would only put him more on edge because whatever he was sensing, he was sensing it. He had lived through these things and he was more sensitive to the movements of how things worked, and he knew how people would operate if they were trying to come onto the property or whatever else. So, I had learned by that point in North Carolina to just let him do what he needs to do to feel comfortable. If you get in the way of that, then you're just going to extend the time of him needing to do whatever it is he feels he needs to do. If people just stepped back and didn't interrupt him, let him do whatever he needed to do, or what he needed them to do, then it would be fine. But, if he got pushback, he would say to himself

'Okay, I think maybe you might be in on this now,' or 'I see you're trying to distract me from looking.' So, there was that.

Something else that was memorable: Sammy was another security person that was there with us and there was this fake gun we had. It wouldn't properly fire but Sammy was playing around with it. I was in the bedroom at the time, John's in the living room with Sammy and I think he was with Ty, the other security. So, he fires it and I hear John, like "What the fuck, Sammy!" I come out of the bedroom with my shotgun, and everybody is looking at me like woah, and I'm like "What the fuck is going on?" Then Jimmy comes upstairs the same way, like "Janice, it's okay." Sammy was like: "It's me, I'm sorry, I'm sorry, I was just being stupid." So that was funny. It was very memorable there, we had a lot of good times, a lot of piano playing, weed smoking, people coming to visit us, and then John and the security fucking with the guests.

One specific example of this: the author that was in the 'Running with The Devil' documentary, Alex, came to visit us and before he arrived John told everybody he wanted them to freak him out a little bit when he came. So, Jimmy goes down there, and Jimmy is a tough-looking character. When he's in security mode and super serious he can be really scary.

So, Alex arrives, they come out with their guns in their hands, shouting "Who the fuck are you, what the fuck are you doing here!?" and they make him get down on the ground, spreadeagled, and search him. Then he was taken to the little cabin at the end of the property, by the water, and held there overnight and I think they went through his belongings. They sufficiently freaked him out.

WHACKD – Do you have any other notable stories from a time you had a guest stay?

Janice McAfee – There was another person that came to visit us. You know, John invited people over all the time, randomly. He would just say "Oh yeah, come on over." So, this person decided to take John up on the offer. He was a really good cook. He cooked these awesome steaks for us, which was great, but then didn't want to leave. He didn't want to leave to the point where John had to get Jimmy to forcibly remove, and escort him, like "Make sure you pack up this shit and leave." At that point, he was just flat-out refusing to leave. It was so weird, so that was one memorable thing.

WHACKD – What events led up to you leaving North Carolina and going on the run with John in 2019? What was it like to abandon everything and how planned out was it all?

Janice McAfee – John had found out that there was going to be a secret grand jury convened about him. He wasn't privy to what specific charges they were discussing bringing against him, but we got confirmation from one of his attorneys in Tennessee who emailed or called informing John that the attorney himself had been subpoenaed to give testimony in this grand jury. The attorney then sent John a copy of the subpoena, and John then tweeted it out. This was about November. I remember speaking to John, and him saying "We have to leave America." I guess because of whatever my face was doing, he said "Well you don't have to come if you don't want to, but I'm going to be leaving."

I gave it some real thought, my brother had just died in November, and they pulled the life support machine, so I'm thinking about that and the fact I would have to leave my kids again, and if we leave, where are we going to go? So, I'm asking him all these questions. "Will I be able to come back and visit my children? How will this work if I decide to come with you?"

I had to seriously consider this because I was also named in the indictment, as well as Jimmy along with three others. So, I'm thinking about it, I still want to be with John and we're still very much in a loving relationship. At the same time, if I leave what does that mean for me?

But I decided to leave. I figured he would be safer if I was with him. I also thought that the only reason I was named in the indictment was as a way to get to John because there was no other reason why I should have been named as a part of the operations of 'Team McAfee.' I had no knowledge of the business side of 'Team McAfee' and they were coming after me for taxes, yet I had no income at that time because I didn't have a paid job, so it must have been just a way to get to John. I couldn't see that they had any legitimate reason, so that's why I decided to leave with John in January 2019.

In the previous summer John had purchased a boat, the 'Freedom Boat,' and there was a massive amount of work to be done to get it seaworthy. By the time January rolled around, it was in a good enough condition for us to be able to sail so we drove down from North Carolina to Miami with our dogs to get to the boat. We had our clothes, electronics, and our guns. We had a lot of guns. We had about thirty different guns because who could we leave them with? So, I thought it was better to take them with us because everything else was left in the house. We sold the house with everything including all the furniture, the TV, everything was sold.

I don't know how I felt. I guess I wasn't so attached to it. I did love that house but by then I was so used to just packing up and moving around that it was just another time having to do that. I was used to moving around even before I met John. I moved around a lot with my pimp. We had a house briefly in Vegas but we were mostly in different hotels. Later, in Miami, there was a nice condo but for me, it was more like a prison. So, I was used to just picking up and leaving, it wasn't abnormal for me.

I was very sad about having to leave my kids, but John made it possible for me to spend two and a half weeks with them before we left. We all went to Disneyland for a week, but by the second day, they were so over it. It was something that my parents did with me, so it was something I wanted to do with them. I went with my sister Loretta and her two kids. We also went to Knot's Berry Farm which was in the same area. It was nice just getting to hang out and make some beautiful memories that I still cherish; this December will be the fourth year of me being away from them. So, it was nice to have that last hurrah with them. I didn't tell my family that I was leaving as I couldn't risk alerting any authorities before we left.

John decided on the Bahamas because there is no income tax there and to be extradited from a country, whatever you're being charged for has to be a crime in the country that you are in, and since there's no income tax in the Bahamas, that's not a crime, and they cannot legally extradite him. Initially, he didn't know what the potential charges were but by the time we got to the Bahamas we found out that they were tax related, so this is why he had wanted to go there.

When we initially got there to Bimini, in the Bahamas, we had all these guns to check into customs and declare, we have all these guns on the table, along with cash and other stuff. The customs agents get on the boat and John shows them all these guns on the table, their faces are like 'What the fuck is going on, who is this person, are you starting a small army, sir?' I'm sure it looked crazy to them.

Then John explained, "I'm running for President of the United States, this is for my security, and these are my guns." He had his spiel to give them and they were okay with that. Then they said, "Well, obviously you can't keep all of this, but you can keep three guns." So, we kept the shotgun, a high-powered rifle and John kept his pistol. The rest were confiscated, the same went for the ammo as we were only allowed to keep a certain amount, but the rest was confiscated, so that was fun.

WHACKD – Now staying in the Bahamas, and later Cuba, on the run in exile, John starts up his 2020 US presidential campaign. Can you talk a little about that time, and what you thought of it all?

Janice McAfee – Well, honestly, it was crazy. He made his announcement on Twitter as we were leaving the U.S. He decided to post about it once we were safely out of American waters but honestly, I wasn't sure how that was gonna play out. It seemed counterintuitive for him to be announcing this, sharing where we were and thumbing his nose at the authorities like that. It didn't seem to be a good idea.

But you know it was good for the campaign, running on the platform that taxation is theft and the fact that he is being hunted for not paying taxes. Which is a misdemeanour, a slap on the wrist and a fine or something. With John's story, he simply hadn't filed and he didn't have a traditional income, he didn't work a job, so how could they know what he owed? They never stated what amount of money they felt he owed, so that's what I thought about that.

Still, it was a very exciting time and the Bahamas were beautiful, that's what I remember most. Just spending time with the dogs on the beach trying to grapple with the fact that we were on the run. I was grieving for my brother and just being away from my kids. Trying to settle into it was difficult. Then we had to hire Bahamian security. Our security from the US had come with us to the Bahamas but John needed them to get money from his bank in America, so John signed some documents allowing them to get it from his bank. Eventually, they came back with $500,000 in cash and brought it to our boat, and so now we have this problem.

There were a bunch of people that knew that we had that amount of money, in cash, on our boat. So, what you see in the recent Netflix documentary of when John and I are on the boat and we're looking under the bed, and we're both armed in that whole scene, well this was around the time that they had just brought this money back. So, any person that thinks critically can understand why we might have been on edge with half a million dollars in cash on board. So, yes, he was shooting on the boat, he was freaking people the fuck out. Hell, yeah, he was, just to let them know "I'm not the one to try it on with if you think you're coming to strong-arm me for my money, it's not gonna be easy." Yeah, that was pretty intense.

WHACKD – What suspicious activity did you encounter whilst you were in the Bahamas?

Janice McAfee – So, when we got there initially, we settled in Exuma. Then we went to Nassau where the U.S. Embassy was. We were trying to get some assistance from them but they wouldn't even let us in the building. A gentleman came out to speak with us but he wouldn't even give us his surname, only his first name and he says "We can't help you," and he turned us away. That was the US Embassy.

Something else happened, which is why I just wasn't comfortable there. I was at this nail salon and the woman there was acting very strange. I had met and had conversations with her before but that day she was just acting strange, she was trying to get me to stay there, and the power had gone out. She was like "This happens all the time, we'll have it back on and I'll do your nails," but it was just weird the way things happened and then this guy showed up, so I just felt unsafe there. I didn't know if maybe their thought process was to take me and negotiate some payment or something. I ended up hitchhiking back because the salon was far away from where the boat was docked. A woman pulled over for me so I got in her car and had her take me back to safety. That happens a lot on the island.

Also, you know, John and I were fighting off and on at the time, he had one of his flavours of the week come, and she was causing problems inserting herself as the 'woman of the house,' or boat. But I stepped back and I said "Oh, that's fine, let her do whatever." I didn't want to be part of it. So, I went to the hotel there, I stayed at Choppy's, which is right there at the pier where our boat was docked. I could see the boat from my room, so I wasn't far away from John. I was always near and I had the puppies with me, our German Shepherd dogs. I just wanted some peace and I think once people were sufficiently freaked out enough by John's behaviour and they knew that he wasn't afraid to shoot, it made people think twice about whatever ideas they may have had about getting his money.

The campaign kind of ran in the background. John had these masks made of his face and he tried to figure out a way where someone could go to the Libertarian Debate wearing the mask while John spoke through a speaker at the debates, but we weren't able to make that happen.

WHACKD – It seems during John's brushes with authority the correct procedures were not always followed in a way that seemed to put John at greater risk, almost like corruption, but with plausible deniability. Can you share any stories that attest to that?

Janice McAfee – Yeah, so there were a few things. In the Bahamas, the US couldn't have John extradited through the legal channels, because like I said, there is no income tax there, so they couldn't legally extradite him. So, their plan became to arrest him on anything, drunk and disorderly, assaults, whatever they could just to get him into custody and then have him shipped back to the US that way. John found out about this and we ended up leaving the boat and going into hiding on the island. We had installed hidden cameras on the boat, so while we were in hiding, we were able to get footage of the Bahamian police coming onto our boat looking to arrest John. Once that happened, we got whatever supplies we needed and we left immediately that same day for Cuba.

It was a good time in Cuba, we went there twice. We stayed in Cuba for the first time for like a month or so because there was a problem with the boat and it had to have work done to it. We stayed there for however long that took, and then we went back to the Bahamas for a little bit. I'm not sure why we did that bounce back, but we did. Once we got back to Cuba the second time, for a few months this time, we were settling in. It's such a beautiful place and the people are just beautiful there.

After we'd been there for a few months, there was someone who came to the boat while John and I were out riding bikes, and they gave whoever answered the door a slip for John that said that they wanted John to meet them. It had the name of the meeting place and the time of day that they wanted John to come but it didn't say why and the person who came to drop off the slip didn't say why.

So, John is informed of this and when the day comes John wants me to go with him. We arrive at this place that looks like an old rundown army barracks, it's a pretty scary place and we're not sure what's going to happen here. Our driver, who was a taxi driver, as well as our inside man to these kinds of things, when he sees the place too, he's like "Oh, I don't know about this." So, he's nervous too, but we go in.

This General comes out and greets John and then asks him to walk with him to talk privately. When they call me over, they say "The US authorities have requested that we send you back to America, but we don't want to do that. However, you have to leave here in 72 hours, you cannot stay here any longer." So, here's another example of where the rules were not followed. There's bad blood between Cuba and America for obvious reasons.

We leave Cuba within 72 hours and we decided to go to the Dominican Republic, mainly because we only had enough gas for that and barely enough supplies. It was such a rough trip; we ran out of water by the second day and the dogs were so miserable. We were all just so miserable. As we began to approach the port, we were so happy to get there thinking that we can shower, eat and get off this fucking boat. But immediately when we arrived at the dock, we noticed all the other boats had been moved to the back of the docking areas. So, there were all the empty uprights for only our boat, which seemed a bit strange because some of the boats seemed to be all packed in together yet there were all these empty lanes.

As we pulled in, there are men dressed in military attire, all carrying high-powered rifles. So, John's doing his thing, he had his gun on his hip, which is something that he always had and we are looking to speak to customs, declare what we have on the boat, and get our passports stamped so we can legally enter into the country, but they wouldn't let us get off the boat.

We were sitting there for hours, waiting, not sure what we were waiting for. Eventually, this man came and asked us to sit on the back of the boat, and we weren't allowed to go back inside. They asked us to just sit there while they are now searching inside the boat. For what, I have no idea. They confiscated all of our phones and then finally allowed us to go to customs but by this point, nobody was in the office. So, we still have not yet officially entered the country. We're also supposed to be meeting some people for some business that John was trying to work out. So, they came and met us like: "What's going on here, this is so strange" So we tell them what was happening and they were trying to call lawyers and find ways they can help us in our situation.

But the authorities took our guns and there was a story in the paper making it seem like 'Oh, we caught McAfee' but at this point, there was no problem with John, no warrant for his arrest, no problem with his passport. He was able to freely leave the Bahamas and Cuba. There was never any issue at all, we never had any issues with moving around. This made what happened in the Dominican Republic even more strange because they treated us as though we were fugitives, although we were kind of on the run from the U.S., there was no official warrant. At that time there were no official charges that we were running away from.

But the boat had been searched then they allowed us to go eat in the restaurant there. They told us that we were all going to some apartment away from where we were, which didn't make any sense to me. I'm like "Why can't we just stay on our boat? Somebody needs to be there with our dogs. Why can't we just stay there? Or why can't we stay at the hotel right here?" It made no sense. John immediately picked up on that and then he faked a medical emergency and they ended up taking him to the hospital and I was able to go with him. I'm not sure where the other guys went or if they were let go, but I do know that nobody was allowed to get back on the boat, which was super strange.

After John comes back from the hospital, they take us to this holding facility where they had all these cells, but they didn't keep us in the cells at that point. We were held in this conference area. We were all together in this conference area for like three or four days and they brought us food every day.

Someone from the US Embassy came trying to find out what was happening and why we were being detained, so John explains to them that we still haven't officially entered the country through immigration and that the Dominican officials were now trying to say that we entered illegally into the country and that we brought our guns into the country illegally. We were still not officially in the country because they hadn't processed us yet, so this was all very strange behaviour. We needed our passports stamped by Immigration, that's how you legally enter a country is by going into immigration and then customs where you declare what you have if you have anything to declare at all. But we were never given the opportunity to do that.

I think we spent four days in that holding facility. After those four days they said they were going to take us to the airport and let us leave, but instead of taking us to the airport, they took us to jail, which was like an old farm or something because the men's holding area was a big barn. The women's area was just a separate area with smaller cells, but you could still see the barn across from where the women were held.

There was another building where there was a set of small cells, and that's where John was with Robert King and the Bahamian security team. All four of them were in there together. In that separate holding area, away from the rest of the general population, that's where the pictures were taken of John in the prison. Even though our phones had been confiscated, I had an old phone in my purse in my luggage. It wasn't any use for calls, but it could connect to Wi-Fi and take pictures from within the prison. Somehow, they had that phone and that's how they were able to get the pictures.

After we spent the night there, we finally went to immigration the next day and they were telling John that he had to go back to

America. That's where he had to go because that's what his passport stated as his country of origin. So, John said "Well, I'm also a citizen of England. I was born in England, and I want to go there. This is against the law and you can't force me to go back somewhere in this way. If anything, the only thing you can force me to do is to go back to where I came from," which was Cuba. And so, there was this back and forth happening with immigration and the lawyers that we were able to get in the meantime. John was in the immigration office and he said "What do I need to do to stop them from shipping me back to America?" There was a court process that had to happen so John decided to fight the deportation, similar to what he did in Guatemala when they were trying to force him to go back to Belize.

Back in Belize, he had the courts intervene, saying "I want to have my day in court, to hear my case." So that's what happened, the courts agreed to hear it and Belize backed off because they were trying to do something illegal. That's the same thing that's happening here now in the Dominican Republic. Once John got the courts involved, they had to back off because everything they had done up to that point was illegal.

While the attorneys were doing whatever they needed to do to get a court date, the people at immigration were telling me and the rest of us that we had to leave. So, John was going to be left alone there, while we all had to leave and go back to our countries of origin that were stated on each of our passports. While the attorneys were trying to deal with that, John came up with the same idea that worked for him back in Belize. To give the attorneys more time he faked having a stroke. It was so funny.

They confiscated John's cash, which had significantly dissipated over those last few months, whilst he was in jail the previous night. And so, they were bringing it back and counting it again, just to make sure it was all still there. Before they started that process, John came back into the room across from where they were going to be counting it and said "Hey, don't be worried, I'm just gonna do my thing." I was like "Okay," so he goes back over to the room. Five minutes later we see him fall face-first to the floor.

I'm like, okay, so now I'm acting. "Oh, my god, what happened? Help my husband, help him. John, are you okay?" I couldn't go over there, so they tell me "Just stay there ma'am, we will get him a doctor." But they are all looking at him like 'Sir we know you're bullshitting, you can get up now' but he stays there, and he's acting. When he comes to, he pretends as though he doesn't recognise anyone. Steve was from our Bahamian security and he was like "Sir, it's me, it's Steve. You know me, sir, it's Steve." And John's like "I don't know you. Get away from me. Where am I? Who are you people? Where's my wife?" and he's calling out for me and it's just hilarious. I'm trying to make tears come but I can't because it was so fucking retarded what was happening, and I'm also not a person that can cry on demand. So, I'm doing my best and this lady was trying to comfort me like "It's okay, we will get him to the hospital." And finally, they let me go to him. I say in his ear "Hey there, they're about to deport me and make me leave for the airport." So, I said goodbye to him, and that was that.

Now I'm on my way to the airport and once we get there a call from the immigration office requesting to bring me back because they are taking him to the hospital. I guess because he's continuing with the "I don't recognise anybody. I'm freaked out. Where's my wife? Bring me my wife."

So, they call and have me brought back. Once the attorneys got a court date and the stay of deportation for John, the Head of the Immigration office came to the hospital and said: "Where would you like to go? John said: "We want to go to the UK." This was after John magically recovered from his medical emergency. So, they bought our tickets for the UK and that's how we ended up in Europe.

Another thing, after those three or four days of being detained, they allowed us to go back and collect some belongings from the boat. They had some soldiers go with us, along with the main person from the detention centre, to the boat, and they asked John to show them where his money was hidden. So, for whatever reason John informed them that he had his money on him because he had taken it off the boat initially. I took a small bag and John took his backpack; he had the money in the backpack so they didn't know that he had the money on him. So, John obliged them and showed them, then we got our stuff and we left the boat with whatever luggage we could carry. I guess they asked because the soldiers had already looked in every possible hole in those initial hours when we were all sitting on the back of the boat, when we were first detained, and they weren't able to find it.

Nobody else was able to go on the boat after we were detained because the dogs were still on the boat and very vicious. The puppies were more so, the other dogs mostly just barked, but the German Shepherd puppies would bite. So, they couldn't have gotten on the boat at that point without an issue. And, again, our dogs were there on the boat this whole time, which was just infuriating. I think that was the most infuriating thing about it. The boat was an absolute mess, there was shit all over the place because our dogs were left alone on the boat the entire time whilst we were detained. I couldn't understand why that was, it didn't make any sense why we couldn't be on our boat. It was just so upsetting, and I'm still upset about it.

After John left the hospital and the attorneys had gotten the stay of the deportation, before we were going to the airport, the attorneys said that they knew someone who could take care of the dogs and that they would arrange all of that for us. So, all of our dogs were able to go to in this place, it might have been a rescue place. This person had a lot of dogs, so it was somewhere they were able to go and be taken care of properly. That was very problematic for me and John, but they were okay, so I guess that's good.

WHACKD – In November 2019 John Created the Cryptocurrency '$WHACKD' and had the word tattooed on his arm, as well as tweeting the now famous 'A la Epstein' tweet. Do you remember any particular conversations you had with John about WHACKD at the time?

Janice McAfee – So, in 2019 he tweeted about getting subtle messages from the U.S. and he had just come up with the idea of the token. He had been wanting to do one for a while and this was an opportunity to have that happen. The fact that there would be a certain amount burned, he got a kick out of the idea.

The tattoo was to put those people that were coming after him on notice and to let there be a public record of this attempt on him.

I think the Epstein tweet came later when he was in prison and it was obvious why he wanted that tweeting out. Being in prison leaves you incredibly vulnerable, as we have seen play out. He wanted to put the world on notice, that if something happens to him, and if it happens in this manner, then know that it was of no fault of his own. Almost prophetically, that's exactly what happened.

WHACKD – Just to go back a bit, in June of 2019, John claimed on Twitter he had 31 terabytes of incriminating data on world governments. Do you have any thoughts or comments on this stuff?

Janice McAfee – I believe that he had that stuff, most definitely. Mind you he had already collected however much he collected from Belize, if that was the 31 terabytes, I don't know.

But we have to remember who John was, the creator of McAfee Antivirus. Now, to stop hackers, which is basically what the antivirus is, you have to know how hackers work, as well as how to hack. He was able to create this product that was number one in the world for however many years, and it is still a very valuable company today, so he was very knowledgeable. How to get information that people don't want you to have or information that isn't public, or that might be behind some firewall? He was very capable of that.

So, I don't doubt that he had information, but who has it? I don't know. I doubt that it would be in any one person's possession, just because that would mean he would have to trust this person very much, and he trusted no-one that much, he only trusted himself. He especially would not put that trust in someone with something that would have been so damning for him. You know, if it was released then his life would have been over, which is why it wasn't released whilst he was alive. It was his ace in the hole. And I doubt that he would allow any one person to have control over that other than himself.

WHACKD – After being deported to England you went off-grid with John around Europe, this was during the coronavirus 'lockdown' restrictions, and can you share any stories from the time?

Janice McAfee – The lockdown restrictions were insane. But John and I were together so it was cool. We watched a lot of Netflix and we were able to have someone do the grocery shopping for us, or John would go sometimes if he wanted to just go out and see what was happening around where we were. He would go to the grocery store with our driver. So, we had all the conveniences, we were comfortable, aside from not being able to go anywhere but watch a lot of Netflix. It was still such a nice time, specifically the lockdown. Just because we were able to be safe and not worry about anyone coming after us, nobody was out in the streets. So obviously that's not the experience everyone had, but it was a quiet time for us.

As was being in Europe, just travelling around. We took a European road trip; we went to Germany and we stopped off at a lot of places. It was just nice because that's how we started off our relationship, with a road trip.

After our first meeting in Miami, about a week later he left and went to Tennessee and bought a pickup truck, he asked me to drive with him to get this truck and then he was going on a road trip to Portland so I joined him. That was an awesome time as well. They say the true test of a relationship is to go on a road trip.

If you can survive a long road trip then your relationship will survive anything, so I always kept that in the back of my mind. Although there were other things in the background, I felt that I was getting to know John, and I liked him. I started, you know, crushing on him. It was just a good way for us to get to know each other. And so, the European road trip was just reminiscent of that, being able to see these places that I'd never been to before. John especially wanted to go back to Germany because he had such fond memories of living there as a young adult, so that was nice, you know him showing me around some of his favourite places. That's also where the video of him in the strip club on the stripper pole dancing happened, in Germany, it was a fun night. Just getting to do, not necessarily normal things, but getting to just go out and not have to be super on high alert, to be able to relax and enjoy being in the moment with him.

So, there are very awesome memories of everything, even here in Spain. We were in Spain for the lockdown, and so even our time in Spain, before he got arrested, was enjoyable. We would go and have breakfast at different restaurants, or dinner, and it was always just a good time. If we didn't do that, then I would cook, or he would cook, which was always a fiasco. Oh, my goodness, he would cook spaghetti and I don't know how the hell he did it, but he would always end up getting spaghetti sauce on the ceiling. What could he possibly have been doing to get sauce on the ceiling? I still don't know. Always the kitchen would be a complete disaster area like a hurricane came through and just destroyed everything. That was just his way, he was kind of like a mad scientist in the kitchen. Everywhere we lived it was the same when John cooked, the kitchen was completely unrecognisable and there would be food and sauce everywhere. I don't know what he would be doing in there, but he was a good cook.

WHACKD – Whilst on the run in Europe John was later imprisoned by the Spanish authorities after his passport was flagged. Can you describe that time in greater detail?

Janice McAfee – Okay, so he had a trip planned. He was going to go to Turkey for some business there. Like I normally did, I packed his backpack and made sure everything he needed was in it. I would do whatever laundry and ironing then leave the clothes that he needed for the day laid out so he had that all ready. That morning, we were sleeping and he woke up early in the morning so we decided to watch a movie. He picked it out. We watched a documentary on Nina Simone. It was a good documentary. I don't know why he picked it out. It was a very serious documentary to watch before he went out of town, but this was something we always did, you know, just hanging out with each other.

So, I told him "Just be safe, I want to know when you get there." There was nothing different about this time. Well, maybe a little different. Just that there was an anxiousness because this was the first time in a long time that we were going to be separated. But I walked him out to the car and said goodbye.

I went for a morning jog, then I texted him to let me know that he landed safely. A few hours later around four or five o'clock the call comes that John has been arrested and detained at the airport. So now everybody's trying to frantically figure out what the hell happened. An attorney was hired by our friends that were assisting us here in Spain. and we found out that John's passport was flagged as stolen, and then a warrant came out of thin air.

John was now wanted for tax evasion. We were just trying to find out where he was being detained because he wasn't taken immediately to jail. I think they kept him in a holding facility at the airport overnight and then took him to prison. Once we found out where he was, it took maybe a week before I was able to get a phone call from him. He was able to have visitors but he thought that I shouldn't go to visit him. It was suggested that it might not be safe for me to go and visit so we had friends that went to visit him. We were able to get a phone number so that he could call me, and he passed messages on to me to tweet for him. That's what he was thinking about, you know. Having his voice heard, it was very important to him. He also had little private notes for me, so I had that.

As far as the warrant, that came out of nowhere. There was no warrant before being detained. There was no problem with him flying and there was no issue with him travelling, going through border control, or anything like that, so that's why I say this warrant came out of nowhere.

WHACKD – Can you share any stories or notable conversations you had with John whilst he was in prison? Did he have friends there?

Janice McAfee – I guess he had friends, everyone in his unit would look out for him. He was kind of a celebrity to them, obviously, but they treated him just like everybody else. They did look after him and made sure that he was okay. There was an incident that happened though where he said one of the other inmates who recently got in there tried acting tough with him, and one of the other prisoners that had been around John stepped in between them, like "No, you go away." So, that ended that. I guess they shielded him from that sort of thing but John was very smart, he knew how to carry himself in those situations. It wasn't his first time being locked up abroad, so he knew how to handle himself. He said that a lot of them were surprised that he was in there, because of what he was being charged with. They were surprised that they were detaining him in general population with all the criminals. So, he was with all the criminals within the common area where everyone else was, he didn't have any special area and he wasn't in some country club, upscale prison or anything like that; this was a real prison. He wasn't given any special treatment, although he was treated with some reverence. The guards would come from different areas of the prison to come in, meet him and say hello, so he had that happening.

Our conversations were only eight minutes apiece and he got three phone calls a day. But I would talk to him about my day, and tell him some funny stories to make him laugh. He would have me collect headlines from the newspapers to share with him so that he was up to date with what was happening in the world. He had me tweeting for him. He would read me his tweets, and I would record them, type them up, and then tweet them out for him.

Here's another notable thing he told me about. You know John was wearing underwear as his facemask. Well, one of the prisoners had gotten some underwear from their significant other and was kinda showing them off. John said that he went and grabbed the underwear and put them on his face as a mask and he said everybody just laughed and laughed. I thought that was so funny.

Other things that happened are maybe not so great. He told me that he felt for the first time out of control like he didn't have any control of the situation. He said that to me in one of our phone calls.

If there was something more happening while he was in prison, he never shared it. He had good days and bad days. There was some stress and he was in a lot of pain. Adjusting to prison wasn't so easy for him because he was older and his knees were terrible, and he was having to do all this walking up and down stairs because they had him on the second level. So, it was hard for him. He also had a torn Achilles tendon that never got operated on and it wasn't treated properly, so he still had that issue. His body was in a lot of pain and they weren't doing much to help him with that. They knew how he was with medical emergencies that he had faked them, so that probably didn't help. I don't know why; they just didn't want to deal with the situation.

A day or two before John died, he told me that he had a premonition and it was really bad. It had shaken him, but he didn't want to talk about it. He didn't want to tell me what he saw or what the premonition was, he just said it was bad. We also talked about other things: the lawyers, what was probably going to happen when we get in court, and the fact that they were probably going to grant the extradition. That was not a surprise; we knew that it was gonna happen. There was already a plan of what to do as far as appealing that decision. We all knew that he wasn't going to be deported the next day, it was going to take time. This idea that he had to kill himself to evade extradition is just ridiculous. That same day, again he mentioned the premonition. We spoke that morning and he mentioned it again, but again, he didn't want to share it with me. I didn't know what was gonna happen. I just knew that premonitions, by nature, are not good, they're usually bad. That stood out to me.

WHACKD – On June 23rd of 2021 it was reported that John committed suicide in jail. How did you first hear the news of John's death?

Janice McAfee – On Twitter, for fuck's sake. Somebody direct messaged me saying "Please god tell me this isn't true." Immediately, I'm like "Fuck," I Google and I see it. I was just inconsolable, absolutely inconsolable.

WHACKD – At the time of this interview in November 2022, Spanish authorities are still withholding John's body. Do you believe John McAfee committed suicide?

Janice McAfee – I don't believe he killed himself at all. I believe that they're hiding something, and they're attempting to continue to hide it. It shouldn't take this long. So, let me tell you what's happening. When John died the prison opened up an investigation into his death, immediately. I don't know if that's normal procedure, but it seems a bit abnormal since the same day he died they released it to the press that he died by suicide, so they had already given a cause of death before there was even an autopsy report. Before his body was even in the morgue, they had already given the cause of death. For them to then open up a police investigation seemed very strange, and it still seems strange to me but anyway, that's what happened. The investigation stayed open from the day he died until February 2022.

At that time, they weren't able to release the body because their investigation was open, so they were going to hold his body until the investigation was closed. I think it was October 2021 when we got word about them not wanting to release the autopsy report. And I said, "We want the autopsy report." Then in February 2022, they announced they were going to close the investigation. At that point, I should have been able to get John's body. However, they were attempting to close the investigation without releasing the autopsy report, as they said we "didn't need it." So, I ask the attorney to appeal the decision about the autopsy report, but I had no idea that meant that they wanted to keep his body, still. I thought that we would be able to get his body, and then do an independent autopsy. But that wasn't the case, and so we filed an appeal in February 2022. After that, I released the petition and people shared it, which helped us to get his death certificate.

I was able to find out in July of 2022 that their appeal process takes six to eight months for them to respond, which is fucking retarded. How long do they need to keep this man's body? How long does it take for them to decide if they are going to release the autopsy report? Why are they holding on to it? I don't understand why an autopsy report is not just released with every death, however, if it's requested, it's supposed to be given. I requested it, but it has not been given. I don't understand why they are not honouring that, or why they are acting against their laws or even just the normal way that they would operate. This is completely abnormal, what they have been doing and are continuing to do.

So that's why we're still here now in November 2022, which is now past the deadline of six to eight months, still waiting for a decision about whether or not they're going to release the autopsy report, which is very important for me to try. Maybe I won't get any answers. Maybe I will never know what happened to John. One reason I want the autopsy report is because, in the police report, I found some very disturbing, questionable things that occurred, that I want answers to. I really can't say more about that, but this is the reason I have pressed for the autopsy report, because of what I have read in the police report. So, at the very least, just know that I tried to gather all the information so that people can be held responsible. Whether he was murdered, or someone gave orders, we can argue and speculate about that until I'm blue in the face, but I would rather not do that. But I do know that it is clear he did not kill himself. I know that much.

WHACKD – I've heard it said that you were the only person to whom John was accountable. I wonder if you've got any thoughts on that?

Janice McAfee – I guess you could say that because I didn't take his shit. To me, he was just John. I wasn't ever starstruck, you know, it was never this "Oh my god, you're John McAfee, you're so much more important than me." You know, there wasn't this reverence like that. No, you're John McAfee, you're a person like I am and you put your pants on one leg at a time just like I do. Now, I respected him, and his wisdom. Obviously, he was fucking brilliant and a genius, but I wasn't kissing his ass. There was enough of that happening around him already, a lot of people swearing their allegiance: "I'll never do anything to hurt you, sir. I'm gonna have your back, I'll take a bullet for you." There was a lot of that shit. I didn't do that; I just came as I was.

If I felt like he was being a little too crazy or reckless I would say something and speak up. No one else did. I don't know if everyone else was afraid to or whatever, but I would speak up and say something because I cared about him and he could take things too far with some of the jokes. He liked to play pranks on people a lot, but sometimes they were not in good taste and he wouldn't always listen to me, but sometimes he would.

WHACKD – Some have compared John's situation to Julian Assange, in some ways. What does John McAfee's legacy mean to you, and how will he be remembered in your mind?

Janice McAfee – I guess it is similar to what Assange is fighting for, or Snowden, or Chelsea Manning, or all these whistle-blowers; I think it's John's legacy as well. People may say he wasn't a whistle-blower, but in a way, he was. Even just through his tweets, he tried to let people know what was happening behind that curtain. Most of us are not privy to seeing the operations behind the scenes in that world. At one point in time, John had $100 million. He rubbed shoulders with a lot of these people, I'm sure.

WHACKD – He did work to expose the financial system for the scam and debt-based slavery that it is. If it's a system built upon belief, he was bursting that bubble.

Janice McAfee – Yes, I agree with that. Definitely. He did his best to let everybody know what he did and to inform people. I would say he was a freedom fighter in a way: he wanted people to free themselves financially, which is why he was so passionate about crypto, and why he wanted to have advisory roles for so many different projects because he knew what it took to be successful.

And that's what he tried to share in his role as an advisor for the different crypto projects, but unfortunately, he wasn't in charge of the day-to-day operation. People were free to take or not take his advice. A lot of them tended not to, and a lot of them tended to be just outright looking to get his money, so there was a lot of that. But that never turned him off from what his goal was, which was to continue to be a sounding board for freedom and to try to wake people up to the reality of their situation.

I think that's what I will remember. Irrespective of what was happening in his life personally, and the difficulties that he had, John always wanted to make sure that he was being vocal about what he believed in, whether it be exposing the corruption in the various institutions, the slavery of the fiat system, or the slavery that we, as individuals, enslave ourselves in working a job that we hate, staying in a loveless relationship, or just living life for someone other than yourself — not doing what you love but just miserably going from day to day. John wanted people to follow their hearts and do what they loved. I think that was his way of seeing things and that will be what I will remember him for the most.

WHACKD – Since John's death, Curious Films have released a documentary on Netflix about John 'Running with the Devil' What is your overall sentiment towards it? And what do you anticipate from the McAfee documentary that is in pre-production by Amanda Milius?

Janice McAfee – Well, with Amanda's documentary, I just hope it isn't the same fucking story. There's just so much more there that should be told. I feel like 'Running with the Devil' was kind of just a sequel to 'Gringo.' They're just focusing on the sensationalism of John. You know, enough already. It's the only thing that the mainstream media talks about, why didn't they talk about everything else? It's as though it's secondary to his crazy paranoia, guns and hookers and all of this.

But who will investigate what he was saying? Who will investigate what he has said about Belize? Who will investigate the names that he has dropped? When he has said that this person is a human trafficker or that one is money laundering, who will investigate these various things? That's the story, right? Who will investigate why the IRS went after him? Nobody, right? Everybody just called him crazy. Everybody just called him paranoid when we initially left America. Who is investigating those things? That would put a target on their back, so, understandably, no one wants to do that.

Now, about the 'Running with the Devil' documentary, I think the saving grace of the documentary is Robert's footage. I think it was amazing to see John, and to hear him, and to just be brought back to that time and place. I do wish that there was more of Roberts's footage, he had so many hours, and he had so much more footage than what they showed there. Maybe there'll be more of it to come in the future. That would be awesome.

And the overall documentary, I guess, was entertaining, but like I said, telling the same story. There's just the sensationalism of it that I don't like because the truth of his story is so much more fascinating than the story they created. It's clear that they wanted to tell a certain story, and that's what they did. Instead, you could just tell his story, from him. Part of my frustration here is that there was enough footage where his story could have been put together. There was enough footage to tell John's story, instead of people telling a story about him, people that didn't know him.

Robert had a different kind of relationship with John from the other people that were filmed in the documentary, but those people outside of Robert didn't know John, at all. They knew what he wanted them to know, and what he wanted them to know was usually something pretty shallow, nothing of real substance about himself, and that's how he protected himself.

John kept a lot of people at arm's length. I happened to get more intimate with him just because I paid attention and asked questions. I wasn't just some dumb idiot fan-girl or just his sex toy, we had so much more than that going on. I got to get a deeper peek into him and to see him a little more. I wish that they would just tell John's story, instead of people telling a story about John.

WHACKD – What do you think people misunderstand the most about John?

Janice McAfee – That he was crazy, because he was crazy, but like a fox. All of his antics had a reason, he was extremely thoughtful and methodical and he knew exactly what he needed to do to get the reaction he needed. A lot of his antics on Twitter were just that, it was a public persona that he created to garner attention so that he could then share his true message. So, the 'Whale fucking' and the 'Eating his own dick if Bitcoin doesn't reach a million.' I bet more people know about that stuff than know about how he truly felt about crypto, the need for decentralisation and the need for privacy.

That's just what it is because we're living in a time when people don't have the attention span for deep thought or critical thoughts. You know, they just want to be entertained. In 30 seconds or less, or a minute or less. If you can't grasp their attention within that timeframe, well they are on to the next thing. John knew how to tap into that and get people's attention. That's a lot of what he did on Twitter, but once you want to skim past all those antics, you get to the meat of who he was and what he thought.

You can see that there is great substance there, and a wealth of wisdom, and a wealth of knowledge that he was eager and happy to share with whomever, with his followers on Twitter and with people that privately messaged him on there. He would spend hours responding to people, and not just something shallow, he would give it real thought and respond to them. That was something I always admired about him, that he would be willing to do that, even replying to people that emailed him; he would spend hours doing that as well.

Some would ask him the same question like: "What should I do with my life?" or "What advice can you give me?" This 12-year-old kid emailed him one time, it was a long email, but he took the time to read it and to respond in kind. That was just his way, he had a love for people and I think people misunderstand that as well.

He had a huge heart and he tried to help people, anyone that he could.

With advice, he was very straightforward and he didn't sugar-coat things. If he told you your project was shit, then it was shit. If that's what he truly believed then he would tell you, not because he wanted to hurt your feelings, but because he wanted you to see where the problems are. He always tried to give fatherly advice, just based on his own life experience.

WHACKD – Over the decade that you got to know John, what did you learn about the world as a result?

Janice McAfee – I got to understand where the movie scripts come from for the movies like Jason Bourne because it was akin to our lives. All of those 007 types of spy movies were like what we were going through. How corrupt the people in power can be and how you're literally on your own. There's no one coming to save you, you have to save yourself and try to dance that dance and keep safe, and keep sane. I got a real education on that.

And it's scary, once you're in their target, you're in their target. But I learned some things and ways how to navigate which can be very stressful. Because of my background, being aware of my surroundings is something that comes naturally to me. A lot of the security aspects were just second nature, like breathing. Oh, that was okay. But, just the intensity of it at times, and the unrelenting nature, you know. By just learning and watching how he manoeuvred through it all, it's not impossible to come out on the other side.

It's just if you're a big enough target, they will come after you. You will be demonised in the public eye. They have to do that for people to dismiss what you're saying outright, but John was able to combat that. With those that were willing to listen, he was able to combat that.

Something that I learned from him is that it's really important to do what you love in this life, because if not, what the hell are you doing? If you're not doing that, then you probably just wasting your time, making yourself miserable and making the people that you're around miserable because you're miserable. So, it's worth finding out who you are. First and foremost, find out who you are, and what you're passionate about, and then try to share that passion with the world and everything will align with that. Everybody here has a purpose that they were born to fulfil. Once you're able to find that, I think that everything else will align, so you'll be able to take care of your family and you'll have money to eat and live and exist, you know, you'll have what you need when you're in alignment with whatever it is that you were meant to do in this life.

One last thing John taught me was to be present, in the moment, at this moment. Not focused on past regrets or focused on the future — whether it's the future you want to have or the doom and gloom of whatever future the news is predicting — just be present right here, right now, and do what you love.

Chapter Two
Sam Dattola

WHACKD – Hi Sam, thanks for doing this. Can you introduce yourself, a little of your background, and when you first became aware of John McAfee?

Sam Dattola – I'm Sam Dattola but everyone calls me Sammy and my background is in the Air Force. I guarded a plane called the Doomsday Plane, which is an aeroplane like Air Force One but its specific use was for times of war. It was an elite duty in the Air Force for which I got a lot of really good training. A lot of the guys in that line of work, whether that be the Air Force, Navy, or whatever else, would go into the private sector, to Blackwater security and I know a lot of people that did that, a lot of my friends did that too.

One guy in particular who did that also knew Jimmy Watson, who was the Head of Security for McAfee, and so he reached out to me after he saw I was posting on social media about crypto, and I'm also what you could call a "conspiracy theorist" or "anti-government" or whatever and so he said to me, "Hey, why don't you send me your resume and I'll get it over to John and at least get you a phone interview." I was like, "Let's give it a shot."

So, he sent it over and Jimmy later called me when I was in Newport Beach, California. I did a two-hour phone interview and we hit it off pretty well, he was like "You need to get a plane ticket to Norfolk, Virginia and I'll pick you up from the airport." I'm like, "I don't know what you look like, I don't know your number, is this a one-way flight? Am I paying for that?" he was like "Too many questions," it was all secretive. But I figured I was just gonna go for it, I took a go-bag, which is where you pack everything up that you're gonna need to live, and I took a one-way flight from Orange County to Norfolk, Virginia.

Jimmy picked me up from the airport, he's this big burly guy, all tatted-up, with a mohawk, and he drove me out to the house in Outer Banks, North Carolina. It seemed like the security guys didn't know each other that well, I don't know, there was kind of a weird awkward vibe, so I was a little nervous about that.

WHACKD – When you first met with John can you describe that event and how you were received?

Sam Dattola – So, after we reached John's house in North Carolina, it was late when I arrived so I found my bunk bed for the night and went to sleep. The following morning, I went upstairs and we were all having coffee and then John came out, I was kinda just in awe. I've been following John's escapades for years, so it was cool to meet him. He gave me an impromptu interview and asked about my experience, he asked me some crazy questions. John always had a way of putting you on the spot and making you feel awkward, but always got to the truth of the matter.

He asked about my arrest record like "What are we gonna find in a background check" so I told him. He goes "Tell me more about this situation where you got into a fight with a cop" so I told him about that. I got into a fight, with a cop, and I was charged with 'assault with a deadly weapon' It was a crazy thing and I was sure he wasn't going to hire me based on that, but he goes "That only makes you more valuable to me." That was when I knew I was going to be a pretty good fit. That's how I got introduced and started with them, from there it was a wild ride.

WHACKD – Can you elaborate a little on your initial meeting with John?

Sam Dattola – So, I was in the living room and there were several people there, I believe Janice was there, along with the housekeeper and four or five other security guys, and these guys were all special forces, and then John came out. He has this presence about him where the whole room is just attentive, aware of him, and you know calling him 'Sir' and stuff like that. He has these piercing blue eyes and a baritone voice where as soon as he starts talking, everyone shuts the fuck up and listens.

John comes in the room and asks me "Are you the Air Force guy?" he'd never hired anyone from the Air Force before, they go for Marine Corps, Special Forces, and Navy SEALs because they're the best at that kind of tactical stuff. He asks me about my military background, and I explained some of the stuff I'd done, he asked if I'd ever driven convoys with a VIP, and so told him how we trained for that with limos, chase cars, tail cars, with VIPs, how to egress Entry / Exit, how to move people around, move vehicles around, what happens if you get into this scenario and that scenario, how to keep the VIP safe, and all that kind of stuff.

After that John goes, "Okay, well, we're gonna be driving a convoy around here, and I want you to be on point." We had these big black Lincoln navigators and we would drive convoy, with one car in the front, one in the back, and John in the middle, typically in his blue Bentley, and we would traverse around Outer Banks like that.

So, he asked me about my experience in the Air Force, about myself, and about my arrest record, and all this was taking place in front of everyone. I was just taking the whole thing in and everyone was carrying loaded guns, at all times, it was an interesting environment.

WHACKD – Are there any particular stories that come to mind from your first week working as John's security?

IN MEMORIAM: MCAFEE REMEMBERED

Sam Dattola – Okay so it was maybe the first or second day there and it was a pretty standard thing that John would go out to lunch, there's a nice restaurant out there in Hatteras Island and so we had all gone there. It was my first time with him, so I didn't know how these things all worked from a logistical standpoint. I mean small logistical things like; where do I sit, am I going to sit beside John, or am I going to take a corner position, or do I take the door to safeguard the room from anybody who might be coming in? I try asking Jimmy and he's like "Don't worry about it, we'll figure it out when we get there," the guy wasn't good with answering questions.

We get to the restaurant and usher John in, he sits at the table in the middle of the room, which is not ideal when you're guarding a wanted VIP, but that's just how he was. I took a table in the back corner with this army kid and there were also a couple of Navy Seals at the front and then John was on the main table with Janice and Jimmy. John then started ordering us all shots of alcohol and I've got an Uzi on me, right, fully loaded. Everyone else has their guns, and we're the drivers, so I don't know what the fuck to do, should I drink this? I look at Jimmy kind of shrugging my shoulders and he motions for me to do the shot, almost to say if you don't drink it, John's gonna think you're a pussy or he's gonna be offended, I don't know.

I did the shot and so did the kid next to me, he seemed fresh out of the army and I just was not comfortable around him, it was as though we were going through a trial-like situation, where we were almost competing with each other, and I could tell this kid was desperate. So, John sent these shots out to everybody and I think it was to see how we behaved, how well we can function after and whatnot, it was a test.

After two or three shots we all got up to leave, we escorted John back to his car and we set off back to the house he started taking all these funky directions to try and confuse us and get us off track but I was right with him, he went down all these crazy turns, down curvy streets and then at one point we lost the tail driver.

We had these two-way radios set up and so he was panicking on the radio and I had to tell him "Dude, we're going back to the house and you need to catch up to us. No, we're not stopping, we don't stop a convoy like this on the side of the road, that's not happening." I tell him exactly where we were and I say "Go fucking 90 miles an hour, go through stop signs" and the guy is panicking. He finally catches up and almost runs into the back of John's Bentley, but he catches up and then we end up back at the house.

This particular house had this long winding driveway that leads up to the garage and John tells us to reverse the trucks, the convoy, into the garage to check our driving skills. So, he goes "Sammy, you're on point, you go first" So I did. The vehicle had a backup camera so there was no problem taking it up the S curves to the top before parking it. Then they told the young tail guy to go up next and so he starts trying to back up and he was going into the bushes, and he almost hit the mailbox.

Jesus, this totally fucked up the kid and he was almost in tears, totally frustrated, I'm just sitting there like "Oh, don't worry about it." But that's little insight into the kind of thing that would happen, John kind of liked playing with people, pitting people against each other people to try and make them compete, for like his approval, I think, it was a trippy vibe.

WHACKD – What was that initial period like working security for John?

Sam Dattola – Well like I said there was this thing where everyone was always trying to vie for John's attention and his affection, it was almost like a constant interview. It was like one of those reality TV shows from back in the day, like 'MTV Beach House' where they would throw a bunch of crazy people in one house and just see what happens, it was like that, but with a little more alcohol and PTSD mixed in, and shit loads more money.

But I knew about John. I knew about his philosophy; I love that he hated banks and neither of us trusted the government. I liked his whole libertarian mentality and I was happy to be a part of that whole thing, I wanted to be a part of it. John was also running for president while I was working for him, so I was a part of that, there were several interviews and podcasts he did during that time that was just hilarious and had some great presidential slogans. He would be getting interviewed by someone and he would just sit there drinking scotch while giving the craziest answers, it was a good time.

WHACKD – How did things develop from there?

Sam Dattola – The next chapter of events I think of as 'musical houses,' which is when we all moved from Outer Banks, North Carolina to Lexington, Tennessee. Just before I turned up 'Team McAfee' had changed the head of security and there was a major drama between this former head of security and Jimmy. By this point, John had given lots of money and vehicles to people and he always put his vehicles and properties in other people's names. It was because of the IRS, lawsuits, and all this stuff, so he tried to keep everything in other people's names, but, if things go bad with other people, then you wind up with major drama.

Anyway, so we moved to Lexington and within a week or two we had an analyst come out to stay, this guy named Luke. I think he was responsible for making most of the money through all the new crypto projects. He would read the white papers and find good ones and then he would reach out to people or they would reach out to him, you know. There were a lot of people that wanted McAfee to pump the value of their projects, and so that's what he was doing for money, they would send him millions of their tokens and he would do a few posts or videos on his Twitter about their project.

If you look through the history of the coins that he promoted they all had this crazy trajectory, and some people made a lot of money, but it was somewhat unregulated back then so you could get away with it, it was kind of like the Wild West, and so he was doing this quite a bit.

So, that's how he was bringing in so much money when I was with him because I was scratching my head before that like I've been around rich people before, but I've never seen anybody burn through money like John. He was buying houses, cars, boats, and jet skis, and he would fly a plane around, it was just wild.

WHACKD – What was one of the craziest things you experienced?

Sam Dattola – Okay, so we are all at John's house and we'd all been out boating and shooting some guns off that day. We got back, and there was kind of a party environment there at the house in North Carolina, but that evening I was exhausted after being out in the sun all day long, so I went to bed early. I woke up to all this clattering, loud banging, and people running, I could hear boots and I was sure we were under attack like the FBI or the ATF must be here. So, I grabbed my gun, lock and load. I could hear people screaming. I'm like 'Oh shit this is going down.' I put my boots on and I rush downstairs, everyone is in a full-blown panic and all I can think is 'What the fuck is going on?' John was on the floor naked and it looked like a cardiac arrest, he was panting, foaming at the mouth and barely breathing.

Everyone was under strict orders by John to keep everything that happened in the house private, don't post pictures, you know, we don't want cops coming around, but this was a fucking 911 situation. So, I'm like "Call fucking 911, he's dying" and so someone did. I went into John's bathroom and on the countertop was a white powder, I knew it wasn't blow because that wasn't his thing. But he did have a thing for something called MDPV, which was his drug of choice, having a binge on bath salts. He had a lab in China that would create the crystals, they would tweak the molecules so that it was always a legal formula and not classed as a scheduled drug. John, you know, he was so smart and so savvy about getting around the law that he would just make a brand-new drug, a new particular set of molecules that weren't a scheduled narcotic on the DEA checklist. So anyways, this was his drug of choice, and here he was now on the floor.

So, there was this drug on the counter in the bathroom so I went and I told Jimmy and the others "Hey, we need to tell the paramedics about this drug because they're coming with the ambulance and the police. I'm not gonna say anything to the police, and the paramedics won't tell the police, but the paramedics need to know how to treat him."

So, they're screaming at me "We're not fucking telling them." All I'm trying to do is save the guy's life. I'm like "Listen, you're worried about legal problems? He's not gonna be alive if you keep this up." But, sure enough, the paramedics arrive and they're like "What is he on?" So, I took one of the paramedics into the bathroom and pointed to the counter, I told him I thought it was bath salts, that he was overheating and having breathing problems, and everything else, like now go do whatever the fuck you got to do. It was such a shit show, and this was just the beginning.

WHACKD – What happened after the paramedics arrived?

Sam Dattola – They get John into the ambulance, which was a fucking nightmare because John's a big guy and he had to be taken down all these stairs on a stretcher, and everyone's in panic mode, all the security guards. There's infighting going on, people are screaming, yelling and tempers are flaring.

Janice was away visiting her kids at the time but somebody was on the phone with her and told her that obviously, John had overdosed and was on his way to the hospital in the ambulance, and then they tell "Sammy told them that he's on bath salts" So she starts calling me right away like "what the fuck did you do?" I said, "Calm down, first things first, they have to know how to treat him and they have to know what he took, this is not about the law, this is not about paparazzi, these medical people have a job to do and they need the information"

So, Long story short Janice asked me to go and grab John's cargo pants, he always wore these cargo pants that were packed with $100 bills, and she said to grab everything off the bathroom counter, especially his shaving kit, but everything in this shaving kit." I knew what that meant, she wanted to get the drugs because she knew John was going to need them when he starts to wake up. So, I grab everything off the counter and grab his pants and all his other stuff and load a bag and throw it into the excursion and we're all racing to get to the hospital. When I got there, I asked Jimmy what was going on, and he looked white as a ghost, he's goes "John's in a coma, and this hospital isn't able to take care of him in the way that he needed." So, they bring in a fucking helicopter and fly him to the bigger hospital in North Carolina, it was like a four-and-a-half-hour drive away from where we were, but they brought the helicopter and

John was taken off to the next hospital, and to the intensive care unit that was on the very top floor.

So, I drove all night to get there and I arrived I was told to hide my gun either in my boot or in the back of my pants, so I did, and then I go up. John was still in a coma and hooked up to a ventilator at the time with all these IVs going into him, John hated hospitals. There was a buzz around the entire building and Jimmy was like "Okay, Sammy, I've been up here all night and I need to go get some sleep. You take over, you're on point now" So, there I was inside the room with John and there was another guy outside, Ty, who was out in the hallway, so we had pretty much the whole upstairs.

So, I'm just sitting there for a few hours and then all of a sudden, he started moving around so I tell the nurse and I think they gave him some sort of shot or put something in his IV then she goes "Let me know if he wakes up" and that "All his vital signs are looking good, he's gonna come out of it." When John woke up, he still had a breathing tube in his throat, you know, he's intubated on a ventilator and he started pulling at the thing. So, I'm calling the nurse to come in, they tell him not to pull it out, but he pulls it out anyway, always non-compliant.

He pulls out this breathing tube and then he turns to me and he goes, "Sammy, where is everybody?" I tell him "Sir. You were in a coma and you're in the ICU. You need to do what these medical people tell you to do. Everything's gonna be okay, you're good. Just leave your breathing tube in." He then tells the nurse to leave because he needs to talk to me in private and so the nurse was like "Okay, but I'm coming back in five minutes."

So, the nurse leaves and John turns to me and in a rough, low voice, he's like "Sammy, go get my cargo pants." I bring them over to him and he's reaching in there grabbing at the hundred-dollar bills and

I'm like "Sir, I can't believe you're fine, we thought you were going to die, I'm so happy you're okay," he's still pulling out these hundreds and then starts throwing them towards me. I'm like "Sir," like what the fuck are you doing, you know, I ask "What do you want me to get" and he's like "I need you to go get me a bottle of at least 18-year scotch." I was like, oh my god, and started with "Sir" before he interjects with "Sammy if you don't get me that Scotch in 20 minutes, you're fired."

So, I go outside and I tell Ty "Go in there with John and keep him going, the nurses will be coming back in a couple of minutes. I'm off to go get some booze for him." So, I get a backpack and head to the liquor store, I get a big, big handle of 18-year scotch and I stick it in the backpack. Now I'm coming into the hospital, no joke, I'm coming into the hospital with a loaded gun and a bottle of scotch. I get to the top of the ICU and I go into John's room, he goes, "Sammy, go get some ice and coke." And so, right there on his hospital tray, while he has all these IVs in, just out of a coma, and he's there pouring himself a drink.

So now he's sitting there with this drink and this big bottle on the side, and he didn't care to hide it. The head doctor then comes in and he knows it's John McAfee, it's kind of a big deal. So, this doctor comes in and there's John with a bottle of scotch on the bed tray. The doctor just stopped in his tracks, looked at John, looked at me, and just shook his head. Then he said, "Well, it's good you've had some alcohol, you've been out of it for over 30 hours and you're probably having alcohol withdrawal, so it's good that you're having a drink because you could have a seizure if you don't have any alcohol."

It's very dangerous to go quit cold turkey like that when you're that much of an alcoholic and have to drink, you have to wean yourself off it. He also thought that someone was trying to poison him, if you ask John what happened, he will tell you that he was poisoned. I also think he was poisoned but by himself.

John also hated hospitals, he didn't trust anyone, and he was very non-compliant. If you're familiar with medical people, they don't like that. So, John's calling over to a doctor and nurse in Tennessee for all this stuff, he wants to be out of this hospital and he wants home care. He's in a hospital bed and he has to be intubated because his oxygen levels weren't high enough, I was thinking how the fuck are we gonna do this? But he's got this doctor and they're figuring it out.

I can't imagine the amount of money all this must have cost, these four days or whatever it was. We had the ambulance to the first hospital, then all that ICU care there, then a helicopter to the second hospital and all the ICU care there, and then, he scheduled a medivac flight to take him back to Tennessee, a jet, an actual medivac jet, with at least a nurse and maybe even a doctor on board. They took John out of this hospital in North Carolina and into another ambulance to take him to the airport. The security team followed and we escorted him to this little medivac jet where we flew into Nashville and John was taken in a wheelchair to his home in Lexington. I scratch my head thinking about how much that must have cost, two flights, two ICU rooms, and two ambulances.

So, he gets home to Lexington and dude it was such a shitshow. He was in the living room in this great big hospital bed and he had this oxygen tank, it was such a battle trying to keep his oxygen level as high as it needed to be. He was so weak that I had to literally walk him to the bathroom, help him go to the bathroom, and help him back to bed. I went from security to a full-time nurse. So, that was one of the most intense things that happened.

WHACKD – Were there other situations during your time with John where the authorities were called?

Sam Dattola – There was a situation, we didn't have a hostage situation, but it was claimed by someone that we did, and so the cops came out and they surrounded the house, so that was pretty wild. So this kid came over, I don't know if he was a podcaster or if he wanted to do some story about John or if he had an alt-coin project or whatever it was, but John was the type of guy that if you caught him at the right time, and you said the right thing to him, he would just be like "fuck it, yeah, come on over", which was loosey-goosey man, and he had a couple of people show up before that were not so cool.

Anyway, so this guy comes out, and he's kind of a beta guy, but he was pretty freaked out because we didn't have any good pre-announcement about what was going on. John was probably on a good one, he might have been on a bath-salt binge, where he locks himself in his room for three days. So anyway, he forgets that this guy is showing up and he has these fucking crazy armed security guards to greet this random dude that shows up at the house. We're all like "Who the fuck are you?" And he's like "Oh, no, John told me to come out"

So, we have this safe room downstairs and he's taken there while we're trying to get information out of John, but he just isn't in any condition to give out the information. There was a guest house right down on the beach, it's nice, so I tell him "You know what, I'm going to take you down to the guest house. You can chill out there until we straighten this out with John, then we can look at sorting your interview " So I take him down there and leave him in the guest house. It was down a long driveway and it's this little house on the beach, kind of on its own from the main house, where we had dogs, cars, guards, and all this other shit going on.

In hindsight, I could see from that kid's perspective, how it could have been perceived that he was being held against will, but that wasn't our intention. I mean, I could see how he was freaked out because there were all these crazy-looking security guys with big guns and German Shepard and a Pit-Bull, and John wasn't around. So, yeah, it didn't look like a safe environment.

The kid was texting some friends and telling people what was going on, they're basically like can you leave? And he's like, I don't think so. I don't think he was the one who called the police but one of his friends did. So, the police needed to do a welfare check and where we were, when they called, we outnumbered the police and out-gunned them. So, they also called in the highway patrol and all these cops were on the main road and they were circling in with long guns drawn and stuff, they didn't want to get too close to the house. At the time we stood out there in the bushes with night vision goggles on watching these guys, like, "Yeah, we know there are people out there. So don't get any closer" kind of thing. Then these cops shout asking about somebody being held there against their will in the guest house. So, we're like "Oh, no, no, he's just waiting for an interview with John" like no big deal. Finally, John woke up and stepped out of his stupor he was like "What the fuck is going on? Get this guy the fuck out of here."

We say to the cops "Okay, we're going to go and walk the guy to his car, we're not gonna have any guns or anything, he's gonna walk to his car and leave on his own volition" The cops are like "All right, we're gonna come up the driveway and meet you at the end of the driveway and make sure that he's okay." So, we're like, "Okay, cool. No problem." We had this kind of whole negotiated exit of this guy, and so he got out of there.

WHACKD – Were there any other situations that stand out in which John was in danger?

Sam Dattola – Yeah, it's funny how something that should be a typical day is just so crazy with John. So, he wanted to go ride jet skis and he had these super high-end, top-of-the-line, big Yamaha jet skis. They were fast, I mean like crazy fast, like turbos, and John drives like a fucking maniac. Anyway, he wanted to go drive them with Janice but she didn't know how to, John also wanted a security guard with him, so I was like "Okay, I'll be the guy, you go do your thing." I look up the Outer Banks you can see where we would go island hopping on these things, there were these cool little bars and restaurants that you could dock up and go have lunch, so that was our thing. Typically, John had at least three or four guys with him for security but we only had two jet skis, so that wasn't possible for these scenarios.

On this occasion, John takes off on one of the jet skis with Janice on the back, and he's flying like a bat out of hell, so we get over to this restaurant and dive bar called 'The Shipwreck' in Hatteras. We had lunch and a few drinks, then we go to get back on onto the jet skis. Again, John takes off like a bat out of hell and he doesn't wait for me, I've still got to secure my gun in the compartment of the jet-ski, lock everything up, and put my life vest on and stuff. But John sped off with Janice and then all of a sudden, I see John flip over the jet-ski.

These are not the kinds of jet skis that you want to flip over, they're just too big, too fast and John was 73 years old, and Janice wasn't an Olympic swimmer. But he flipped this thing over and I'm like "Oh fuck," I didn't even have the jet-ski ready and all of a sudden John's waving and screaming, drowning. I have to decide, if I take my jet ski it could float away, So, I'm like fuck it, I'm gonna swim. I literally swam about 100 meters out and grab Janice and get her back to the jet-ski, then I grab John and put him on it too, he's like "What fucking took you so long?" I was like "John, I had to make a bunch of choices and that was the fastest one."

John gets back on the jet ski and he shoots off back home, way faster than he should have. I swim back to the dock and get my jet-ski and try to catch them up. John already gets back to the house and did a terrible job of tying up his jet-ski, it was almost about to float away. I sorted that and then I tied up my own and when I got to the house everyone was just sitting there looking at me, all the guys were looking at me like 'What the fuck happened? I was like "What did he tell you?" the guys reply something like, "They said they were drowning and you took way too long." I have to defend myself and I go "No, Mr McAfee, Sir, the quickest way for me to get to you in that scenario was for me to swim, so that's what I did. I pulled you both out of the water and onto the jet-ski, If the rescue took too long you wouldn't be telling me about it right now" John just starts laughing and he's like "Okay."

Now, this is typical McAfee, I went downstairs where all the vehicles were and he had this Rubicon Jeep, he had just gotten it and it was really nice. He takes the keys to the jeep and throws them to me and he goes "Here you go, Sammy." I'm like "What do you mean? Do you want me to move it? or wash it?" and he just goes "No you can have it; you did a good job today." So, he gave me a Jeep.

WHACKD – Did you ever have any serious problems with any of the other security staff during your time?

Sam Dattola – In Lexington, there was a little bit of friction in the household, at this particular time it was because of Jimmy Watson, he was fucking crazy, and he was quite an unbalanced guy. There were a couple of scary dudes there but Jimmy could be very scary. There were some crazy stories about him towards the end like he kind of went mad, running off into the woods during a rainstorm and John's telling me to go find him, I'm like "fuck that."

So anyways Jimmy had a wife, Leah, she was a pretty girl, very cordial, very polite, southern girl and we would do grocery store runs. John would be like "Okay, Sammy, you and Leah go to Costco and load up on supplies for the house." So, it was nothing out of the ordinary. So, we went and then come back to the house and unloaded everything. Jimmy then calls me into the living room and he's like "We need to talk."

I go into the living room and he's saying "What's up with you and Leah?" I'm like "What the fuck are you talking about? And he's saying "Are you trying to get at my wife?" I tell him I would sooner put a gun in my mouth than try to pick up his wife. Right, when I said that, he had a pillow on his lap and he moves the pillow over to show he has a fucking gun, he's got his finger on the trigger, and he's now pointing at me. I go "Jimmy, don't fucking do that, you have a military background, your special forces. Are you fucking kidding? You're going to point a gun at me? I'm not fucking around with your wife. I go get groceries with her, I talked to her, we're friends and I've done nothing disrespectful, ever" So, he goes "Well let's keep it that way." From that moment on I thought okay, I need to keep a distance. But he got worse, dude. He got worse and worse. He had a full meltdown and ended up in some safe house for Blackwater lunatics and we had to go get him, I mean, it was gnarly. He's got some serious baggage. I mean, I'd have a hard time living. I would probably be either finding God or finding the bottle or I don't know.

WHACKD – Can you share what it was like leading up to John escaping the US to go the run?

Sam Dattola – It was crazy as usual. John got word through his vast network of people that look out for him that the IRS was closing in on him so he knew that pre-emptively and had this big yacht called the Great Mystery, and he planned to sail away. He could get a nice place in the woods off-grid and lay low, but that was not John's plan. He planned to get into the yacht with three dogs, three security guards, a Captain, and Janice. Personally, I thought was a stupid plan because you're going through customs, you're going into ports and that's the worst thing you could do. So, looking at this whole scenario I'm like 'No, I'm not gonna do that.' An 80ft boat gets small quickly. I did talk to Tommy Austin and Ricky who went with them, and it was not a luxurious situation, I'm glad I wasn't there.

Before John left, we all had to start liquidating everything. He wanted to get rid of the house, the cars, the boats, the jet skis, and all this other stuff, so we're trying to sell everything. I started calling my investor buddies in Orange County and stuff but man, if somebody followed John around and picked up the details of all those deals, it would be mind-blowing. He would buy a house, like the one in Tennessee, he probably bought that house for $800,000, and a year later it was sold for $400,000. Then the one in Outer Banks was a beautiful house, God I wish someone could have got that and turned it into a BnB or something, I don't know what it sold for but he had all these beautiful classic cars, houses, and vehicles that were all sold so cheap.

John didn't have any appreciation for money, he had no respect for it. Money was always just far too easy for him to acquire. He just did whatever he felt at that moment, he didn't give a fuck. He would just go do his thing, he was John McAfee and people would just be like "Okay, we got you."

I think he also had at least one Russian oligarch that was a real fan of his, almost cult-like. John would reach out to these different people, or they would reach out to him and they would just send him money or say 'Go stay in my hotel' or whatever. That's how it was, he was always pretty well taken care of like that.

WHACKD – Did John share any particularly memorable stories with you about his past?

Sam Dattola – John told me all kinds of crazy stories about his past that were fascinating. There was a time when he had this big, crazy mansion that he built in Colorado, up in the mountains, like up in the mountains, and he turned it into a yoga retreat and he wrote a book about it.

I read a little bit about him online and then some of the stuff that John told me was just so interesting, there were so many different things that John would do, and it was like, you just get bored of it, like 'fuck this mansion, fuck this retreat.' but the way he described it like he had all these students or whatever they were, coming to the retreat to learn from him, learn yoga, and the lifestyle of meditation or whatever the hell he was doing. Typical John, he was probably banging half the students.

It later dawned on me that it was almost like a cult, and then I started thinking about how we all were and my life with John. I looked up the definition of a cult, and I think I might have been in a cult, I mean, everyone there would have killed or died for him. He could say anything and people would be like "Uh huh, yeah," even really smart people I saw, they're just like "Okay yeah, let's do that." Certain rare people have this heir, this energy, that just magnetizes people and he was one of them.

WHACKD – Did you witness or experience any other senses of real danger? if so, can you elaborate a little on those incidents?

Sam Dattola – I was probably about a month to five weeks in and I knew it was more dangerous than anything I've ever done and I'm an adrenaline junkie. I don't get scared easily, but I knew how dangerous the environment was that we were in, John liked it that way that's just nature. I could tell by that point how unpredictable and maybe sort of desperate, some of these guys that worked for him were. He brought in a couple of guys that were just... Jimmy Watson had his issues and I didn't trust him, but there were so much worse. There was one kid, I could see he gonna fucking lose his shit, and he did, this is the kid I mentioned earlier. We had just fired him and he was having a full-metal-jacket moment in his car. I thought he was gonna come back in and shoot the whole place up. I sent an email as a written notification to my friend like if anything happens to me, I don't know which one of these people did it, but I did not kill myself.

There were some crazy motherfuckers there, honestly, there were times I was working through a mid-shift, let's say three or four in the morning and I'm out on the couch with my Shotgun, or my Uzi or my nine mil, or all of the above, and I'm supposed to be protecting John from the bogeyman. Sure enough, John is the bogeyman. He's in his room, coming down from a three- or four-day binge on bath salts, he's totally paranoid and possibly hallucinating thinking that someone's either trying to get in the house or out in the field.

John had like 10 locks on his bedroom door, as soon as I heard those locks, I was like, 'fuck' because you don't know what you might be dealing with, the guy might come out and just shoot me. So, I would just get up and go to a lit-up area with my hands right where he could see them. I would be like "Hey, Mr McAfee, can I get you something to drink?" but at any moment I was going through my head about how to defend myself, or how to escape.

One time in Lexington I had to put a chair up against my door when guns were shooting off in the house. I was laying in the bathtub while they were firing guns inside the house. So, did I ever feel a sense of real danger? yeah, there was, quite often, it was very dangerous.

WHACKD – Can you share any little-known stories about attempts on John's life, or did you know at times that he was in danger that may not be as well publicized?

Sam Dattola – I'll begin all of this with 'he thought.' There was a guy, who was from the Wolf of Wall Street, not Jordan Belfort but his partner, and he was in some sort of convoluted deal for the yacht. They had some sort of falling out. When John had that overdose or poisoning and was hospitalised, he thought he was poisoned by that guy, that was the guy we got the yacht from. Then something else happened where the yacht was stripped of everything inside of it, someone stole everything and he thought it was that guy, and it could have been.

WHACKD – Do you have any other stories with John you wish to share from before he went on the run?

Sam Dattola – There was one time this guy came, Charles Nadar, and he had a project called Docademic or MTC which we were all pretty heavily involved in, I don't know if we ever made much money from it but Charles sure did. He was a congenial guy, a good-looking guy, he had been on the cover of Forbes magazine in Mexico and in Spain and he has this super up-and-coming project, crypto, an alt-coin project that was supposed to do big things, I don't think it ever did anything. We all got some MTC coins so I always checked in on it but it was one of the things where it went up, went down, and never come up again. But Charles was out there when we were in Nashville, Tennessee, and we were all staying at a hotel and we're having this big meeting with Charles because we're going to do stuff with his project.

Something happened, John drank too much or something, and Charles showed up as our VIP, we got this nice hotel and stuff so John was like, "Hey Sammy go take him out on the town, go out to eat, and then go to the strip club, get him drunk and then bring him back here and we'll do the deal" or something like that, I'm like "yeah no problem, I can do that sir." So, I go out with Charles and we go around Nashville, go to all these little bars, and go to the strip club and then Jimmy starts calling and I don't know what his problem was but he's like, "Get your ass back over here, McAfee is ready for the meeting what the fuck is taking so long?" I'm like "Dude, I did exactly what you told me to do. What's your fucking problem?" There was a lot of narcissism at play and a lot of egos.

So, we get an Uber, me and Charles are pulling into where the hotel is, and fucking Jimmy Watson is out front and he's got his gun in his hand as we're pulling up to the hotel and he's like pacing back and forth, looking like he's about to lose his shit. As we pull in, he comes up and starts asking the Uber driver questions about where we were, and what took so long and he's tapping his gun on the guy's car. I'm like "Jimmy, what the fuck, Charles is here and you're over here talking to this cab driver with a gun in your hand and tapping on the fucking door of this guy's car, are you fucking out of your mind?" And he obviously was.

When we went up to the hotel room McAfee had an attitude towards me after whatever Jimmy had put in his head so was like 'You know what, fuck this.' I jumped in one of the navigators and went to Lexington, which is a couple of hours away from Nashville. I was literally about to pack my stuff up and take that truck all the way home. I mean, it wouldn't have been stealing because it wasn't his name. I thought at that moment, I was over it. It was just too tribal and too clicky. I mean, when it's bad, It's so bad and when it's good, it's fine. I was making good money but at that moment, I was ready to go.

When I got back to Lexington, Ty was there and he was the voice of reason, he was in special forces, in the army, and he was a nice guy. I was packing my stuff and he's like "Sammy, you don't want to do this. There's good money to be made, we need you here." Like "don't just bail, just calm down, smoke a blunt and just chill, pretend as if nothing happened." So, I'm like "Okay," It's almost like being an abused wife or something, like 'Okay, we go back and just pretend like that didn't just happen.' So that was one incident.

WHACKD – What led to your departure from the role of John's security?

Sam Dattola – There was another incident when Charles was there and McAfee was pissed off at me because I shot an air gun off the balcony of the house in Hatteras, North Carolina. Those guys were shooting real guns and I shot an air gun, but John was like "You're disarmed for the day" and he told me to take Charles Nader to the Virginia airport and he's just going off on me, so, I was like "You know what? I'm just gonna keep this vehicle and I'm gonna leave about that."

He's like "You're done," and he's threatening me "I'm gonna kill you," "I'm gonna call the cops"

I'm like "Go ahead call the cops, the vehicle is not in your name, you're threatening to kill me and you're a fucking psycho. Do you want to get cops involved? I didn't think so."

Then Ty gets involved again and he's like "We're going to go negotiate you leaving." So, I tell them "Okay, the Jeep is in my name, give me my crypto, give me my cash. Give me all my belongings and a plane ticket home and I'll go, so that was kind of wild.

WHACKD – Was that you're final conversation with John?

Sam Dattola – I was back and forth with John on social media, but I texted him some pictures that I had of him and Janice and some goofy pictures of me and him flying a kite, and then I was telling him how it was a great experience, you know, how I appreciate everything, and I hope that he's safe and I'll pray for him and everything like that, because I knew that he was going through some crazy shit and he's like, "you were one of my best guys Sammy, I hope that everything's okay with you and if you ever need anything, let me know." So, it was cool, John and I were cool, and I actually really liked John. He's a fascinating human being.

WHACKD – Is there a particular story that fascinated you the most?

Sam Dattola – I'll tell you one more story that I think is interesting that John told me. So, before McAfee Anti-Virus he was working for the train stations in St. Louis, Missouri, and he was programming the railroad tracks to be safer and more efficient. So, he was doing all this programming stuff and he was also going through some crazy stuff with his wife at the time, he was just in a bad space in his head.

He had gotten a hold of some kind of drugs, I don't know what they were but he told me this story and I know John, he doesn't have any reason to lie. He told me that the drug he had, most people would take a gram of, and he took an ounce of it, which is typical of John. I don't know if it was acid, bath salts, or what it was, but it was some kind of hallucinogenic or psychotropic drug because that's what he preferred. He said he lost his mind, as in completely insane. He said he lost his mind for an extended period, to the point he was going to have to be taken care of.

He said he remembers being on a park bench plotting to kill his family, his wife, and his kids, that's what was going through his head. He had lost his mind. Then a Mormon guy approached him and started talking to him. He said the conversation with this guy lasted for several hours and then he slowly started to feel his sanity coming back to him, this was before McAfee Anti-Virus. He told me pretty much his brain came back; he was intelligent again and had all his faculties. He also said after that event he didn't have any fear or ego.

When I look at John, some of the stuff that he did, and the way he interacted as he did, rules did not apply to him, he just didn't give a fuck. He didn't care what people thought, he didn't care what societal norms were, he didn't care what laws were, the guy just didn't give a fuck. So, he told me that story and I looked at how he is, how he behaved, and how he lived his life, and it was like 'wow, I'm pretty sure that's true. He lost his mind and it came back like pieces of a puzzle, but the fear and ego just weren't there.

John was very interesting, if he likes you, he could be the most generous, funniest, interesting, charismatic, and most genuine person in the world, but if he doesn't like you or doesn't trust you, oh, man, you don't want to be on that side of the coin. If you cross him or if you're on the other side of that path, not good.

WHACKD – In June of 2019 John claimed on Twitter, he had 31 terabytes of incriminating data on world governments. Do you have any thoughts?

Sam Dattola – Okay, he did tell me about that. The word was that you know, he had backdoors in McAfee computers, in government computers, and that's true. I know for a fact. He said that he had all this stuff on Bill and Hillary Clinton, and that whole, you know, there was a lot of stuff about human trafficking and drug trafficking through the Caribbean, and through Belize, which is very believable and for sure that stuff is happening, and so It's very believable that John does have that stuff.

He did tell me that he had it, and he made it sound like it was on a dead-man switch, meaning that if something happened to him it would all get uploaded via some surrogate, I don't know who, and to WikiLeaks. That was his insurance. But that was something John talked about a lot. There were times when I had one-on-one conversations with John that were very lucid, and it seemed to me like he was being very honest, he had no reason to lie to me.

WHACKD – Do you think John McAfee was WHACKD?

Sam Dattola – So, if you want my opinion about the suicide thing, being that I know John very personally, I don't think that he would commit suicide. I just know that John is a fighter. He isn't afraid to live in squalid conditions, he's done it intentionally at times and he's not someone who has to be pampered. He's not going to kill himself because he's in a jail cell.

John is a fighter and he loves the fight, and that's a big fight. He was going to get a lot of attention from all the court stuff and I think he would have relished that, there was no reason for him to do that, from what I know about John, he wouldn't do it.

WHACKD – During your time with John, did he change your outlook or perspective in any particular way, and if so, how?

Sam Dattola – Well, I was already heading down the red-pilled path, meaning not trusting the government, and John just solidified that, he personified it. With his whole libertarian way of thinking, it's exactly how I think it should be. Get the government out of our lives, live and let live.

WHACKD – What do you think people misunderstand the most about John?

Sam Dattola – Well, I think that we have a perception here that people have to put off a certain image to be taken seriously in politics. But, when you look at whom we have in the White House right now, what a fucking joke. The guy can't even walk, he can't even read off his cue cards. He's disgusting in every way and he's groped other people's children publicly, John McAfee would be 10 times the man that he is in the White House.

John McAfee was very honest about his drinking and his drug use and all the crazy stuff. He was very honest and out in the open, he's so honest that people didn't want to take him seriously, and I just think that's sad. I would much rather deal with an honest man than the kind of scumbags we have right now.

WHACKD – Do you have any other comments, stories, or quotes from John, you would like to share?

Sam Dattola – Well, one funny little anecdote. Well, there are so many of them. He used to play the piano and I think he would just kind of freestyle and he was great on the piano, that was always really fun. He would also talk to the dogs which I found interesting because he would talk to them, he was very well convinced that they understood him, and he understood them.

I'll say this also, I'm 55 years old. My life has been interesting, it hasn't been boring. I've travelled all over the world.

I've done all kinds of crazy things. In the one year that I spent with McAfee, nothing compares. Nothing at all.

Chapter Three
Robert King

WHACKD – Hi Robert, thank you for taking part in this. Can you introduce yourself and re-tell when you first became aware of John McAfee?

Robert King – My name is Robert King. I'm a photo-journalist and filmmaker. I first met John McAfee in 2012, when he was on the run in Belize. That was my first introduction to him and his story. I say that because I grew up with Norton. I was on a Macintosh system so I wasn't familiar with the antivirus software on the DOS.

WHACKD – When was your first direct communication with John, and how did that come about?

Robert King – I was doing a lot of work in Syria at the time but I popped out of Syria to meet the Editor in Chief at Vice. During the meet and greet, an assignment came up and I was asked if I wanted to accompany Rocco, the Editor in Chief of Vice, to Belize, to document John McAfee, who was wanted for questioning about the murder of his neighbour Gregory Faull.

WHACKD – When you arrived in Belize and met John, what was that like? How were you received?

Robert King – There was a big lead-up to meeting John, so we were kind of excited, you know. The story is about to happen. An unknown van is gonna pull up, the doors are gonna open and we're just supposed to get in. We didn't have any indication that McAfee would be in the van and considering where I came from, that's kind of a red flag.

But there we are, then the doors open, and there's John. We got in, and he was very cordial, he was with Samantha and another girl, Amy. There was also Keith and the driver, who didn't want his name to be known. John was very kind and very polite and so we started introducing ourselves, showing him a few publications and stuff. We had just published the Syria edition of Vice Magazine so we were showing him that, letting him know a bit about us, and then he began to relax a bit.

So, we were vetted, and he starts enjoying himself and playing games. Remaining in disguise he begins to talk about what was going on in Belize, with Anonymous, about shutting down a site in Belize during that time. It was weird, you know, and the weather, it was insane.

WHACKD – What stays with you the most from that initial van ride?

Robert King – That van ride was odd, not in the sense of how he disguised himself, but more how the media didn't fact-check the information that McAfee was feeding to the outside world from inside that van. Just from his phone, making calls and posting stuff on websites, saying that he had been arrested and stuff, they were all just reporting this as fact. Then, maybe two days go by, and they all think McAfee's in some remote prison in Mexico when we're already heading up the Rio Dulce in Guatemala, where we spent the night in a hotel.

It's not my job to tell the wires they got it wrong, just because I'm a member of the press. I'm on this story and the guy is just playing the media. I'm just the camera guy on this. I'm not affiliated with Vice, other than doing some stuff in Syria at the time. It wasn't my call, nor was it my responsibility to inform the wire services that I was with John McAfee, while they were searching for him in prisons across Mexico.

So, that kind of sets up the geodata leak, but that's what was going on. And we were interviewing John, him reading in the van: "John McAfee has just been arrested." It was some good footage.

WHACKD – Whilst documenting John on the run from Belize are there any little-known stories or memorable moments from that time?

Robert King – There were some interviews, obviously, but no, I didn't have that kinda exclusivity with McAfee at the time. You know, it was funny seeing him eat this steak, all alone at this big table. He had ordered food for I don't know how many people and everybody had got up already, he's sitting there, the media just outside the doors you know, flashing their lights, the attorneys trying to hold them back, and he's just sitting eating this steak.

So, at that time, I had no connection to McAfee, other than me being there trying to figure out how fucked I was after the Geodata leak. So, we weren't buddies at the time, we knew we were in for a shit show, but that's also why I think he was so kind: how he allowed me to kind of clear it up in the end.

WHACKD – It is alleged that John donated computers loaded with malware to the Belizean government uncovering conspiracies leading back to the U.S. did you have any conversations with John about that?

Robert King – There were and he said it publicly a lot of times, that he gave computers with keystroke logging software to the government of Belize. He had uncovered a plot, and he uncovered child abuse of a sexual nature. US diplomats, he claimed. I don't know at what level. Then, he found out that Hezbollah from Iran was flying people to Belize, obtaining Amish or Mennonite passports of dead people, then infiltrating through Mexico to stage a ricin attack inside the United States. This was published all over the world, you can still find it but nobody in the US reported on it. Even where I live, there was a karate instructor, I don't know his name, but he got busted for manufacturing ricin the same year that McAfee made it back to Miami. I don't know if it's related or not, but then fast forward and McAfee is living in Tennessee, so who knows what was going on.

It was later on that he told me that story, when we were in Portland, Oregon, whereas in Belize I was just making videos of the correspondent, interacting with the subject. So, I didn't have alone time with McAfee, other than when he was right about to get arrested and I just happened to be present with my camera. As soon as Rocco could get downstairs, he was there. But overall, it was only like four or five days, you know, it was quick.

WHACKD – During John's escape from Belize and subsequent arrest in Guatemala, it seemed that many authorities were involved. You and Rocco were holed up in a hotel and possessions were confiscated from your room. Can you describe any of that in greater detail?

Robert King – Well, that's exactly what happened. McAfee was arrested, there playing the flute when he was about to be thrown in jail, but that was what was going on. After we filed, we went across the street and discussed that we'd got to get a copy of the footage out of the country. We got to make a copy, you know, then mail it before we leave here. We didn't want to come up short, that's not a part of the business plan. It's being a journalist, you can get to the story, make the imagery and get the footage, but if you can't get it out, you're not doing your job, and that's a big part of it. So, we were talking about that, and then John was arrested.

Then, Rocco and I were locked in the hotel arguing with Vice. We knew that the authorities couldn't enter without a warrant, so that afternoon I ordered room service for a masseuse to come to my room. Rocco was hanging out in my room that day, and that's the only reason my shit wasn't stolen too, but the receptionist at the front desk informed the thieves that my room was occupied, you know, I was in the room.

Maybe they were watching the camera systems, I have no clue, but Rocco's stuff was stolen and taken to McAfee's prison. We were talking to John, he's getting cell phone calls out of the prison, and Rocco's trying to get his computer. The reason we were able to leave the hotel is that I wrote to Guerrera, the Attorney General, saying if our passports were not back by the morning, I would release footage of him taking our money and passports, with the intent of getting our entry stamps from an illegal entry, so just give us our fucking passports. That worked because we got our passports and then felt somewhat safe. We sure as hell didn't want to get picked up without any documentation. At least we had something legitimate in case something else happened.

WHACKD – Are there any common misconceptions people have from that time in South America that you can clear up?

Robert King – You know, I didn't know him during that time and he never told me the definitive story of Belize. He would talk about developing ointments from the plants in the jungle, but that's already known. It was some sprayable you know, self-healing ointment that speeds up the time your wounds heal, like minor cuts that could lead to infection. He was looking at that type of stuff.

I tried to get him to talk about crypto to see if he was involved with it at that time, but he wouldn't answer it. Then I said, well "What year did you buy your first cryptocurrency?" And he said, "I don't remember the year when I first had sex." So, you know, he wasn't gonna answer my questions on that topic. And then later when I'm on a boat in the open seas, I wanted to stay on the boat. I don't think that he was keeping me from asking hard questions, but it would prevent me from overstepping my role, as you know, as a documentarian.

WHACKD – After returning to America from Belize in 2012, John was able to reinvent himself and began to engage in US politics. What did you make of this and his subsequent 2016 US presidential run?

Robert King – You know, the Libertarian Party, the independent ticket, it's needed. We have a polarised two-party system, where political identity is kind of relatively new to this country. What was always country first is now party first. McAfee was a threat because the division in this country is almost fifty-fifty, especially in the last few elections. Even if John had gotten four or even two percent of the popular vote, or the electoral college, if he won one state, he could disrupt the outcome of the whole presidential election. Unfortunately, that's a threat, rather than an opportunity to create a platform of negotiated compromise, or at least negotiation.

But he was able to reinvent himself, partly because of the media storm and publicity that he received while escaping from Belize which he was able to capitalise on. He was already a known media man from his early days of selling antivirus software, and then his yoga retreat. He was a bit of a newsmaker, he owned newspapers, he delivered papers as a child, and being a part of the media was a part of his life from early on. Nonetheless, I think a lot of the publicity that went around that time was beneficial for his stature.

To rise again from having everything burned down, being kicked out of a country and wanted for questioning, then he finds enough financial support to run for president, it's a beautiful thing, I think, to be able to do so. I think he ran an honest-to-god campaign too.

WHACKD – Before John left the US in 2019, John got deep into crypto, he campaigned that taxation was unconstitutional and challenged the US government publicly in many different arenas. Do you have any personal stories or highlights from those years that you can share?

Robert King – After 2012 I left Vice Magazine. John had started running for president when we got back in touch, I was living in Germany at the time helping to create a video department for BILD, the tabloid. So, when I came back to Tennessee, McAfee was living nearby where I lived so that's when we first began our relationship on a more personal level.

That was around 2017 and Bitcoin had already been around for a while. It was the early beginnings of the Coinbase app, just when crypto started to become more accessible. I had just returned from Germany at the time so I didn't have much going, but John was investing in crypto mining so I was playing catch up, asking him about cryptocurrency, with no idea what I was doing really, but I was trying to get my house up and running. Then he got indicted. It was MGT capital. I think there was this guy that claimed to be a Google exec, and he basically defrauded everybody, used McAfee's name like many and just pillaged.

So, it was in between that time. I had stayed with him in Tennessee for a few days but it got a bit crazy for me, and you know, I lived there, and I've already had legal issues in the state. I didn't want to revisit anything from my past in the state that I know so well. So, that was a part of me not being around in Tennessee, and I had other things to do as well as family stuff.

John, Janice and I would go to look at boats on the Tennessee River, or close to it on Duck River, and just weird stuff would happen. You know, he was a bit paranoid, already shooting up a bunch of shit, in the house.

The only reason I mention that is that in Tennessee, word gets around quickly. Let's just say this: if you're not on the right side, you'll die. I think he was a bit over the top for Tennessee. He called the sheriff and told him "If you're going to roll up on me, you call me ahead of time, so my armed guards don't shoot your officers, Mexican cartels are after me." Now, whether that's true or not, I don't know if that's the right way to call your local sheriff.

WHACKD – After John left Tennessee in 2017, do you have any other stories you would like to share from that time before John left America?

Robert King – Well, he left Tennessee and moved to North Carolina and then the indictment came through in 2019. I don't know why he left Tennessee. He probably got tired of it. So, he was in North Carolina, doing great, getting ready to run for his election and second presidential campaign. He was in a better space and seemed happier.

He had done well in his crypto endeavours too. He built himself up as a kind of superpower within the crypto world, and he was a leading voice and a supporter of noncustodial accounts. Now, he made some outlandish statements about Bitcoin going to a million but, you know, whatever. But he was a mover and shaker in the industry. And he did nothing wrong, cleared of all charges from his time in Tennessee.

WHACKD – What events led you to go on the run with John for the second time in 2019?

Robert King – John tweeted that he was running from the IRS, he didn't want to pay any more taxes and that he was tired of it and he wasn't getting the services that he deserved for the millions he paid. I called him and asked if I could visit, and he said "Come on." That's when he said he was going on the run for the second time. I said, "Can I go?" He said, "Yeah, come on."

I drove up through the mountains at night, highway 129, called the Tail of the Dragon, all the way in Hatteras. I mean it is far. Then you just leave your car there and hope to fucking God it's there when you come back. Even then, you have to figure out how to get there again to find it, I mean, there's no airport around there and it's like a $100 Uber ride from the nearest train station. You know, it's far, man.

WHACKD – After John tweeted that he was leaving the U.S. he dumped all his assets and left North Carolina for Exuma. What was that like? What events led up to your subsequent arrival in the Bahamas?

Robert King – Well, him packing up and having to say goodbye to his last place in North Carolina. It was sad, boxing shit up, giving shit away. Knowing it's all gonna be gone as soon as he drives out of the driveway, it was hard. Then, having to take out whatever cash he could get per day from the bank, which took a while. Whatever, he was gonna go. It was sad he had to leave again. He had reinvented himself in the crypto world after Belize, but he was on the run again. In the beginning, we just kind of went dark. We kept our cell phones off and chips out.

We got to his boat and then went to the Bahamas. It was just a lot of driving, a lot of long hours in the car. We had to go all the way from Miami, halfway up the Eastern Seaboard, so it's a few days drive. Shit, just to get out of North Carolina took a damn day from where he lived.

WHACKD – John was running for president from exile on his yacht. What did you make of John's 2020 presidential run? Can you share any memorable stories from that time?

Robert King – To see John reinventing himself on social media, I was impressed by how he could operate pretty much on Twitter and not rely heavily on my services. You could make a whole documentary just off his damn Twitter page. He would use some of my videos, but it was easier for him to just turn the phone on himself than it was to call me into the room, have him read a monologue for 30 minutes then have me edit it down to two minutes, you know.

He would write out his two-minute speech and then time it with the timer, go through it a couple of times, make sure he got it right, and leave a couple of seconds in the beginning and the end, in case you need to clip it, and he would do it himself. All he needed at that time was Janice to spell check and some grammatical stuff. It was amazing to watch this man reinvent himself at least two or three times since I'd known him. I was just inspired by it, so running for president in exile seemed like a pretty good gig.

I don't know what happened, though. They wouldn't allow him to debate via Skype or Zoom to participate. He was gonna have an imposter clone speak for him but he had to be there in person and he felt if he went to the US he would be arrested. The libertarians wouldn't allow him to participate if he wasn't in the arena on stage. Once he found out that he couldn't even register, the campaign kinda went nowhere.

WHACKD – In June 2019, John claimed on Twitter he had 31 terabytes of incriminating data on world governments. Do you think this was potentially the same data from Belize?

Robert King – Well, I don't know. I know he had data on Belize. And again, I think a lot of people would send him data too, whether to get confirmation or just to get him in trouble. He wouldn't divulge that or who may have been sending out whatever it was he was getting, but obviously, something was going on.

As to who holds the data, I have no clue. I never saw a hard drive with him or a thumb drive that he claimed had all the evidence to take down world governments. Whether he had it or not, he was a big part of the internet community. He had white hat hackers and black hat hackers as his allies.

He was well-regarded in the hacking community; it would be silly to think that people wouldn't offer him their finds.

WHACKD – In the Netflix documentary it was revealed that whilst high on bath salts John had shot holes in the boat, feared that people were hiding on board and drew his pistol at you. What do you make of those events in retrospect?

Robert King – Well, you know, it was all true. John was a big supporter of bath salts. I didn't think that drawing the pistol out was the worst of it. Other things were going on. You know, you had a vacuum shift with the security change on the boat. It was nuts, man. A lot was going on and there was more going on than just what was on the boat.

I mean, yeah, he would shoot on the boat. He discharged his weapon because he was afraid that the security had rendered their firing pins inoperable, so that's why he was shooting on the boat. It's a .223 and he's shooting it at a 20-gallon bucket of sand. That ain't gonna fucking hold. It's just rule number one: you don't shoot in the fucking boat. You want to go to target practice, take the motherfucking weapon outside, go shooting and come back, but I believe that was the thinking, and it happened a lot.

People were not very settled at the time. Remember he just left everything and he was always shaking his security. He always did. I mean that's just part of the method: don't keep people too close. You keep your security detail fresh because the security can rise against you when they know everything about you, and all your dirty fucking habits. And he was a bit paranoid, you know, not like a tyrant, but you see it in leadership. You shuffle your cabinet in any form of leadership, and he treated his security as Cabinet members.

But you know, fuck, I did bath salts with John. So, I don't feel like there's a problem talking about it because he talked about it, and you know, and it was legal shit. They weren't the bath salts that you get at the fucking gas station. You can order it by the kilo and they can't do anything because it's legal. That was the way it was so I don't feel like I've betrayed anyone's trust, you know. There was a lot more shit that didn't get in the doc, but there was no holding back.

John was alive, and not in jail when he contacted the company Curious Films, or Curious Films contacted John, and John made the agreement with them. But once he died, you know, I wasn't gonna demand a re-edit. I felt that it was honest enough. It's not meant to be flattering, it's a fucking documentary, but it was honest enough to bring light on the injustice of his death. I mean, honestly, I felt shocked. His life story ends with him getting killed in a fucking prison.

And if you take the geodata history, my history, where I'm being accused for almost a fucking decade of leaking the geodata on him that got him arrested, it brought light to that too, so I felt that it told a true story. I didn't see the final edit and it was John that made the deal. He called me to release the footage to them, and I did what

John asked. I liked the film. You know, I released the footage and that was that. I gave them everything.

Now, when he pulled the gun on me, he didn't even point it at my nuts, he pointed it at my fucking toes. Maybe there could have been an accidental discharge, whatever, you know. It's not the first time somebody's pulled a gun on me. He didn't slap me over the head with it. He didn't pull back the fucking trigger. It wasn't in an aggressive way. I didn't find it aggressive.

WHACKD – The documentary seemed to imply John drawing the gun towards you was the reason for you departing from John, but I think you ended up in jail with John. They messed with the timelines a little in the documentary.

Robert King – Yeah, so I left after, I had to get the footage out. It was getting crazy. We're in tight spaces, they're organising Bahamian security. I'm arguing with the security personnel of John and Janice's, and they turned on me. One night I'm hiding, sleeping upstairs. I barricaded myself in and they came running with something long, covered up in a beach towel, a long beach towel, looked like a fucking stick in a beach towel, yelling my fucking name at sunrise.

So, I slipped out, got into a fucking cab and went to the airport, it was so early. We were all paranoid, you know, we were partying. So, I'm in the airport and I speak to this lady. She's walking in and sees me all pacing and freaking out, so we're talking and she goes "Where are you coming from?" I told her and she goes "Oh, my brother owns that yacht club, why don't we give them a call?" So, she calls them and they convinced me to come back and I did.

Then we hung out, you know. I didn't leave that abruptly. I came back, we had a few more nights and it was good. I went back home to attend my son's high school graduation. After reviewing everything and trying to pitch it to different people, making edits and stuff and not getting anywhere, I went back on my birthday. I stayed there for a month maybe a few more weeks than that, then we were kicked out of the Bahamas. It was weird. He was about to get collected, so we left and then engine trouble forced us to the Hemingway Marina in Cuba. Before that, we stayed at another place in Cuba. I can't remember the name, but then we stayed in Cuba for almost two months, and it was amazing.

WHACKD – Do you have any little-known stories from that time in Cuba you can share?

Robert King – John raising money in the back bars of Cuba selling crypto, and just counting the cash. He raised like $150,000 in three days and that means he probably raised more because he had to convert it all into dollars, you know, so he was getting just shit tonnes of Cuban currency for foreigners, and then figuring out how to get dollars out of it. Just to leave would cost like $30,000 in fuel for like half a tank, so after Cuba, we spent a few days at sea and arrived to enter the Dominican Republic where we were detained and deported. So, yes, I did spend time with him in jail, and it was really important to get that footage because at the beginning of our relationship, I was accused of leaking his fucking geodata, and that brought a real negative black mark against my whole war correspondent career. That matters because I photograph not only future kings, presidents and vice-presidents, and senators, from laymen to soldiers. That's not my job, providing geodata, that's for mortar teams.

It was very important that I smuggled my cameras into the prison and remained in control of my fucking hard drives. I probably can't go back to the Dominican Republic now, but there were no charges. I'm a journalist, not a weapons smuggler, and that's what they accused me of being, you know, so they're already going after me. I mean, can you imagine? I've already had Interpol on my ass because of Ukraine. And then all this shit in the lead-up. I mean, it's just nonstop, and I don't know what they did with that information. But I don't smuggle weapons. I use them in Tennessee, but that's about it. No, that is it.

WHACKD – What events occurred between the initial arrest in the Dominican Republic, and the subsequent jail time?

Robert King – Well, before we got to the prison John banged his head really hard. The seas were rough, so we were in the hospital for two days. There was also an incident where the authorities were trying to pick him up to force him into an unmarked vehicle, right as he got off the boat. There were also a lot of people in the crypto world there waiting for him. It was really weird, you know. He just supposedly got the Epstein dump, and then there are all these crypto people trying to help him out, but once they realized we were getting arrested, they leave.

We were kinda in limbo between the jurisdiction of the port, which is the Navy, and whoever was behind our detention. We demanded to get our shit off the boat, you know, our possessions because I had hard drives hidden in the boat. There was a VHS tape slot in one of the TVs, so that's where I put my hard drives. They dropped down nicely.

So, while we're trying to negotiate to get back on the boat to get our shit we sit down at a restaurant and just order like a gallon of vodka and some appetisers, we just continue to get drunk and inebriated. Then, they allow us to get back on the boat. John had a ripped Achilles so he couldn't really walk well, and as we're trying to get to the boat this unmarked van pulls up demanding that John gets in.

At this time, I can't film. I was filming a bit on the side but I didn't want the cameras to get taken, so I was kind of hiding them. We all demand that John gets taken to the hospital and not put in the unmarked vehicle, and so he gets some CAT scans. He did hit his head hard. I mean we were behind the wheel and the seas were rough, it was bumpy shit, man. They took us to this immigration centre and told us that we'd be staying there for a couple of nights. Then, they said we can leave, so we're all leaving, we get in a van, and we're taking pictures with the guards, you know, being nice. We're all together. Then they take us to prison. We were expecting to go to the Antilles or somewhere else, you know, and then collect the boat or whatever, but that's not the case, we go right into the prison system.

WHACKD – How was your experience within the Dominican Republic prison system?

Robert King – Well, we weren't in the general population, we were detained with everyone that was on our boat, except Janice who was put into gen-pop, but they took care of her. So, we didn't have any other people in our cell except us, all the males from the boat, in one cell, locked up.

Within five minutes, we were passing notes down to the other prisoners and John already had the prison guards on the take, bringing us chicken and Pepsi, smoking proper Cubans in prison. I don't know how, but he figured it out so quickly, it was crazy.

WHACKD – How were you able to smuggle the camera into the jail?

Robert King – I mean, literally that $150,000 got counted like 20 times, and that's how I was able to do it. They didn't check for computers or cameras or anything. I mean there were silver bars worth thousands, so it looked kind of gangster, but whatever, it wasn't. And the real money, the cash, they just kept counting it, so that's how I got the cameras. They were too busy looking at counting the money and it was dark. It's the third world, you know, it wasn't a very lit area.

The money was an issue that started when we left Cuba. Now, we've got three or four days on the open sea, with real strangers, on an $800,000 Buddy Davis Sport Fisherman, a million-dollar boat, with $150,000 in cash, and to top it off we have to cross through Haiti. It would have been easy to disappear in Haiti, so that kind of freaked everybody out, but then we got arrested in the Dominican Republic.

WHACKD – What happened after being released from the D.R. jail?

Robert King – Then they deport us. We were accompanied by, I think, the Dominican police. They hand us over to Customs and the Customs guys gave the Dominicans a harder time than the Dominicans gave us. We didn't do anything wrong, nonetheless, we were deported now.

Then, boom, John shakes his security and he shakes the team. I don't know how Janice got to the UK. John claimed that he used his British passport and then he picked up new security. Then he was left in the European hands, obviously, not as free as you may want to believe.

WHACKD – Did you have any communication with John when he was off-grid in Europe?

Robert King – We had a few Skypes, and he was having a good time. We were planning on linking up but then he went into the Faraday cage, so I knew that was done. It was easier to link up when he was in America, but yeah, we spoke.

We also spoke on the phone when we made the deal with Curious Films. John was in Europe when he made the deal. Whether they reached out in London and made the deal I have no idea. But when he reached out to me to contact Curious Films, I believe he had already left England. I don't know where he would have been, there were so many speculations on where he was.

There were also rumours that he was working on the Catalonian Bitcoin, and if you're dealing with Catalonia, it's not going to go down well with the Spanish government, especially if you're trying to create an independent currency. I don't know the details, you know, I just know what he posted on Twitter of his new bodyguards and stuff and the strip club.

WHACKD – Do you remember what your final communication with John was?

Robert King – Well, I think the last communications we had was, we have this, like mad cow disease in our deer population, it's called Chronic Wasting Disease, and so I was talking about having to decapitate deer heads so the state can test the brains of the animal, and how, you know, how I was turning into a savage, but that was about it.

Then, someone reached out to me while he was in prison, which I doubt was him. So, you know, I responded in kind. So, the last time I spoke to John, we talked about deer hunting.

WHACKD – As a man who experienced war zones for a living how did you find transitioning from that to documenting John on the run, twice?

Robert King – Well, the second time around it was a part of clearing my name after the geodata leak, you know, not being a liability to others on the battlefield. It was out of John's kindness and grace that allowed me to clear my name in the profession that documents death, the horrors, all the pain and the suffering, all of that, as a document to the unanswered on how did this happen? Or who did it? I needed to be allowed to clear my name. I think John recognised that I wasn't responsible. And that was kind, he didn't have to do that.

I mean, that wasn't my only reason. I came back from Germany and this is what I have left in my archive, then Covid fucking hits and that's that, man. I still have to eat, and this film opportunity comes up, so I take it.

Yes, I mean, the shooting on the boat and shit, that brought back a lot of tension. You know, brought back a lot of bad old memories and childhood memories. It was in tight quarters, man. A lot of shit, a lot of moving parts. A lot of emotion. And you know, having to leave everything. And then, playing that chessboard trying to replace the security that you brought with you for the unknown local security. Can they guarantee your safety? Being able to operate on another level; those are dangerous paths. Money is your only vehicle when operating in those types of environments.

I'm using my combat knowledge to know when it's time for me to get the fuck out of town and pop back in when things have settled down. It wasn't out of fear. Some instincts told me "Robert, take a break, go see your son finish high school and then come back," you know. I was editing what I had, and there wasn't enough. It was close. It wouldn't have been my edit either, that film. That's why I like it. You know, I wish it had more stuff, but there will be more John McAfee films, I'm sure.

WHACKD – What are your thoughts on how the recent Netflix documentary used your footage ultimately? Does the final product do justice to your work that spans over a decade?

Robert King – I don't think it was about me. I became the vehicle to tell the story because he died in prison. You know, Curious Films were given the opportunity, and that opportunity was cut short by the murder of John McAfee. They still had the deal in place and we had to tell the story. I was just merely one of many people that helped tell that documentary. I wish they had used more of my footage, you know. It was shaky, it was quick, I like how it opens up, where it kept to the integrity of the DSLR shooting video. That movement, that freedom, you know, opening up your aperture and everything, it was beautiful.

And, if I did my own documentary, I couldn't tell the story of the geodata and make it sound anything less than a 'feel pity for me' kind of documentary, and I think that Curious Films were able to eliminate that danger, so I'm happy with the footage. There's a lot more of it, of course. I wish it was a mini-series, but he's gone and it was over a year, and they still hadn't allowed the release of his body — still haven't. This is not normal. He's an American, he's British, and this is a European prison. Since when are they so fucking barbaric? Two and a half fucking years.

WHACKD – Will there be any further material of yours released in the future? Or is your John McAfee archive now in the ownership of Curious Films?

Robert King – I own the footage. It's only leased to Curious Films, and it terminates when the film disappears from Netflix. So, why do another film? It's done, it's the documentary. There's no reason to release it. I mean, I'm happy with the documentary. It brings to light the issues that we're dealing with right now, about how they've treated an American-British citizen, in Spain.

WHACKD – In June of 2021, it was reported that John committed suicide in jail. Do you believe he was WHACKD?

Robert King – I think he was killed. Yes. Absolutely.

WHACKD – Do you have any further comments on Janice's situation with the Spanish authorities withholding John's body after all this time?

Robert King – It appears to me that the Spanish government is holding up the release of the body. Nobody's touched the body besides the coroner. I didn't know their embalming fluid was so good. What do they do, soak him in old wine or something? How are they keeping his body preserved? So, I think he's gone. There's every reason for people to want him gone, from anti-Americanism, to not paying taxes, to being the oldest or the richest guy in prison, to putting on a prisoner's girlfriend's panties on his head. There were a lot of things that could have gone wrong for him inside that Spanish prison.

Being picked up by Interpol, it's already hot. You're in Europe, you're on the Red List, then you're in jail and it's a rough prison and everyone's afraid to talk about it. And the cartel, you know, they're arresting cartel members. All these things. Google 'Sinaloa.' Fuck, if you Google all the elements, then yes, there's the probability that he was murdered, and the way they're treating his body is another indication that something other than suicide took place.

There was no indication that I was aware of that he would commit suicide because he would be deported to America. Hell, the charges were dismissed anyway, and even if he was fined it would have been $100,000 or less, you know, under $200,000. For John that would have been easy. He could make $150,000 in the bars of Cuba in three days. Just get him to America he could do it in 12 hours, if not less.

I don't know what to say about Janice's situation. I don't know where she is, we're not in contact, and if she's keeping it on the down low,

I want to respect that. I speak to the press and the media, but, you know, all I do is make films and photos, I'm radio silent.

WHACKD – Over the decade that you have known John, in what ways did he change your outlook or perspective on the world?

Robert King – Yeah, the fact that you can keep reinventing yourself. I admired how he was able to explain things in layman's terms, like with crypto. Another thing was his kindness, but also the brutality of the powers that be. It's hard not to compare his situation with Assange. With his body, it seems like they're just punishing people. I don't know, it's hard. Why would a government show the dark side like that? I still want to travel back to Europe, but man, it scares the fuck out of me. What do I have to do, put on a Ukrainian patch or something?

I feel like all this is an opportunity but also a tragedy, a real tragedy. It is not okay, what happened, but the silence is painful in itself too. It's like nobody gives a fuck. Poor Janice, you sympathise with her, and her desire to bring light and truth to the circumstances surrounding his death. Let's say John could pay the Spanish authorities to escape and live a reclusive life, well, how corrupt is that? I mean, any way you look at this, it's corrupt. That's what's so disturbing.

WHACKD – Do you have any other comments or stories from John that you'd like to share?

Robert King – I think I've shared enough. I mean, he fought for everybody in many ways, many times. I saw him at some of the kindest moments of his life. He was more of a statesman and an elder. I'm a fan. I don't mean to say it like that, but he was an inspiration.

Did he change the course of my life? Maybe made it a bit more difficult, it didn't open any doors. We had to fight to get where we were. If anything, you got tainted. Tainted and fucked with. And it doesn't leave. There are a lot of coincidences in this life, and the relationship that we had, they probably weren't coincidences, I'll say that much.

Chapter Four
Chris Rice (RiceTVx)

WHACKD – Hi Chris. Thank you for doing this. Please introduce yourself and describe how you first became aware of John McAfee?

RiceTVx – My name is Chris Rice, I'm the host of Rice TVx, formerly Rice Crypto, and I'm a content creator. I have three different shows on my channel that cover a wide variety of topics. I have 'The Rice Crypto Show' for crypto and blockchain, 'Rice Report' for politics, economics and current events and then 'Stranger Than Fiction' for fringe topics going down the rabbit hole of conspiracies, talking about law, spirituality and a lot more.

I've been familiar with John McAfee for some time. I'm a little bit older than some of the people in crypto. I'm in my late forties, 47, to be specific, so I was around when the antivirus programmes came out, so I was very aware of the McAfee name growing up.

It wasn't until maybe 2017 that I saw the documentary on Netflix: 'The Dangerous Life of John McAfee, The Gringo', which is a bizarre, bizarre story. It got me attracted to the man, the myth and the legend.

WHACKD – How did you find yourself in the orbit of John McAfee?

RiceTVx – Fast forward just a little bit. I started my channel in January 2018 and in the fall of 2018, I started working as a contributor with World Alternative Media, which had over 100,000 subscribers. At the time my channel had fewer than 1000 and World Alternative Media brought me on to contribute in various ways. One of those ways was hosting interviews, so that's how I got connected to the very first interview with John. Jimmy Watson was working with Team McAfee at the time and he got me connected with Janice. Soon after that, he stopped being a part of Team McAfee so I just spoke with Janice directly after that point.

One claim to fame that I have, and I wish there was more competition for this, and that John was still alive, but I did have the opportunity to interview John McAfee more times individually than anybody else. Now, Mark Eglinton had the opportunity to spend a lot more time with John, but they were a different kind of interview with it being for the autobiography. The Bad Crypto Podcast was right behind me on that with five interviews, but since then I did those interviews with Janice. As I was telling you earlier, I've had the opportunity to work with Janice for several months helping to coach her and get her prepared for interviews so that she would be able to answer all the questions appropriately and at the same time, do justice for John. Janice really wants to make John proud with what she's trying to accomplish. I mean, John was so well received and did well in interviews so she wanted to make sure that she was giving the same sort of quality.

WHACKD – Before being in contact with John, what memorable moments from his life come to mind?

RiceTVx – Well, the wild bizarre crypto stuff, the whale fucking, the "I'll eat my penis if Bitcoin doesn't hit a million dollars by 2020," that kind of came later. My first memory, you know, it's rather disgusting. Going back to the first big Netflix documentary about John: he was living a very interesting life. When he was in Belize, he had several girlfriends, younger ladies that were of age, and he was taking care of them, and he had some crazy sexual turn-ons. It was something to do with faeces. So that was one of my earlier memories. But the whale fucking was probably one of my favourite moments. He had a great sense of humour.

WHACKD – Do you know if that was true? I know it was claimed in the documentary, but do you know if that was true?

RiceTVx – No, well it's one of those things, you know. I mean I asked John a lot of questions and I had an opportunity to get kind of intimate, but I never really got into his sexual preferences with him. It kind of makes sense though, in a way. I was a gentlemen's club DJ for 19 years so I've seen a lot of psychology in that area. If you're an individual who has a lot of power, for some reason some of these people, to even out their life, as far as the power, and giving up power, it's kind of like a degradation, the whole getting shit on by girls helped to even them out. Because you know, you see that with a lot of people and not just men, but higher profile people at higher pressure jobs. It's a sick world we live in, my friend.

WHACKD – In 2018, you had your first interview with John, he was promoting 'economic freedom through cryptocurrency' and using slogans such as 'Don't vote for me'. What did you make of it all at the time?

RiceTVx – I thought it was a bold move. It was one of the reasons why I wanted to cover the situation and kind of get in his head, try to find out what the thinking was behind his madness. Like, why did he want to run for president? Then researching it I found out he ran before I was fully aware of who John McAfee was. He ran in 2016 for the President of the United States Libertarian Party. He was doing it to bring attention to cyber security issues. Then when he decided to run again in the 2020 election, he was doing it to bring attention to cryptocurrency.

He said he knew he wouldn't win, but he wanted to still have his voice heard, which I appreciate because it ignites a flame that hopefully inspires other people to do similar things. Why would you waste your time running for president knowing that you're not going to win? The driving factor was getting his message out, and having his voice be heard. Something really drew me to that idea.

WHACKD – Were there other notable moments around that first interview?

RiceTVx – The very first interview went well. Something I did this year, in 2022, was to release some older interviews as 'Rice Rewind' episodes. I talked to Janice to get her permission. Even though I could have just done it, I still wanted to have her blessing. So, I had a lot of unreleased footage from all my interviews with John, I compiled all seven interviews together along with the unreleased footage that people didn't see, including stuff that was cut out from before, and after the interview originally aired.

In the very first interview, two awesome things come to mind. One, I introduced myself to John before we officially started the interview. I was recording and my cat started doing something in the background so I made John wait for like a minute and a half while I went to tend to my cat. I realised in retrospect when I was putting the edit together for the 'Rice Rewind': I was like "Damn, I made John wait for me for like two minutes," which is kind of a ballsy move, that being my first interview with him. I'm sure people don't make John wait like that.

The second cool thing, now, I did not take advantage of this even though I should have, as Janice told me "If John said it, he meant it." He invited me to come out to his house. He was in North Carolina on Hatteras Island, where he had lived before going on the run. He left from Hatteras Island in North Carolina to go to the Bahamas.

The first interview was before all the charges, and John was running for president, from North Carolina, and he invited me to his home.

Three months after that interview, maybe a little bit more, a little less, he goes on the run. Had I known everything, in retrospect I would have just made plans and gone to see him. I didn't think he was really serious like that, you know.

But yeah, making him wait because of my cat and then having him invite me out to hang out, even though I never actually got to physically hang out with him were the notable moments from the first interview.

WHACKD – Not long after your first interview, John and Janice fled to Exuma in the Bahamas. John continued his presidential campaign whilst in exile. Are you able to speak on that time and the indictment that forced them to flee?

RiceTVx – We didn't go into a lot of detail on that and there wasn't much public information out there as regards the IRS charges. The reason he chose to go to the Bahamas specifically, and this is something that John taught me, was that if you commit a crime in one country, and you go to another, if that second country doesn't recognise it as a crime, then they can't hold or extradite you for the nation in which the crime was committed.

So, in this case, the Bahamas does not have an income tax, they don't believe in the taxation of labour, and therefore they couldn't officially be extradited by the Bahamian government to the United States. Because the Bahamas don't recognise laws regarding income tax, there was no crime.

WHACKD – Do you know of any details of John leaving the US to go to Exuma?

RiceTVx – No, this is more of a cloudy area. This was a time when John was offloading some of his assets and doing it in a way that wouldn't have the IRS retrieve or freeze his assets or funds. I think like under-the-table deals. Now I don't know if this is 100% accurate, but I've heard that the house on Hatteras Island that John owned, I heard Jordan Belfort bought it.

There might have been some sort of agreement that said like call it $10,000 or some ridiculously low figure and then John might have got paid $100,000, like an under-the-table deal. I can't confirm it was Jordan Belfort, but there were properties in Tennessee, properties in North Carolina, vehicles, and stuff like that were all sold off. I think he had a little bit of notice, but ultimately, he didn't want to have a situation where he was going to be held by his assets.

John wouldn't have had a problem with prison if there weren't all these other exterior threats on his life. Being in prison makes it easier for someone to take him out. You can incentivize prisoners quite easily, and we're talking like cartel stuff, it's a completely controlled environment. Well, depending on what side of the fence you're on. A lot of those correctional officers don't make a lot of money, so it's really easy to corrupt them and entice them with bribes too.

WHACKD – It's easy to look the other way too, like "Go on a break, don't worry about it."

RiceTVx – Exactly, and with John going on the run saying that taxation is theft, especially the way that the United States is doing it, that takes a lot of balls. We don't have very many people like that today. There's been some who have done comparable things, you know, Julian Assange, there are some parallel people, but John was a special breed of his own in that category. He got people thinking and questioning things, whether or not they got the answer or not, at least it got people's brains ticking a little bit, which I think is one of the most important things, planting seeds.

WHACKD – When John was in Exuma, still running his presidential campaign, the Clone McAfee paper masks were an interesting tactic. Do you know of any other tactics like that used in his campaign?

RiceTVx – He was very public about things at that time. There were a lot of people who went to visit him, like Anthony Pompliano. A lot of people that I knew went to visit him. That was a unique situation. The only reason he ultimately left was because of corruption in the Bahamian military. They were trying to set him up in some capacity for the US government. He got notice ahead of time and he took off to Cuba.

Something that I didn't know, though. I thought his journey was from North Carolina to the Bahamas – Bahamas to Cuba – Cuba to the Dominican Republic – then to England and off the grid. But I found out it was North Carolina to the Bahamas – to Cuba – back to the Bahamas – back to Cuba – to the Dominican Republic – to England – then off-grid, which most of the time was apparently in Spain.

WHACKD – What was the reason for the Bahamas – back to Cuba – then the Bahamas?

RiceTVx – I don't know if he was just checking things out, but it was before John got any sort of notice about the military situation in the Bahamas. I can't say I remember every single thing that's taken place, but I'm very knowledgeable about the majority of it. I can fill in a lot of blanks, but I don't know everything, unfortunately.

WHACKD – On June 9th, John tweeted that he had 31 terabytes of incriminating data on high-level officials. Do you have any thoughts or comments on that?

RiceTVx – Yeah, a lot. I asked Janice over the time that we spent talking about it. I believe it exists. In what form or where it's at, I can't even begin to even think. Has the information already been given to authorities? Are arrests underway and we just don't know about it? We don't know what kind of incriminating evidence was on there. I don't see any ties to Q or the Q-Anon stuff, and I don't see John releasing this information methodically on a blockchain, putting up tickers on a web page saying the information is coming out on such and such day, or such and such time. I don't believe that.

One interesting thing from around the time of John's death, there was an apartment building in Florida that had a weird incident take place, that took out part of the building. Some people were claiming that John had a son who had an apartment in that building, and that's where the information was and that it was where the building was damaged. Ultimately, they ended up taking down the entire building because they said that damage had caused structural damage to the rest of the building. They just tore it down. I found out that information was false, though, in that John didn't have a son that he recognised as a child.

WHACKD – Yeah, there was some stuff circulating at that time that claimed to be from John's Twitter saying something to the effect of "My 31 terabytes of data are in that Florida building." It was just a fabricated tweet though.

RiceTVx – That might be the case with the son story, trying to create some sort of conspiracy out of it. I believe that John was smart enough that if he had this, he probably gave the information to people and was like, you know, upon my death, get rid of this. I think that's also possibly a reason or one of the reasons why John's body hasn't been released.

This is something that Janice mentioned in the interview, that got me thinking. Is it possible that they're trying to keep this idea that John's alive so that whoever does have the information, it makes them apprehensive about releasing it because they're not sure if John's dead or not? Not just that, the fact the Spanish authorities haven't released his body. You know, why isn't Spain releasing it?

WHACKD – It's all very suspect, and the Telegram groups claiming to be John, any comments on those?

RiceTVx – I completely discount them. A lot of people took advantage of John and his name. I've seen some of the stuff that's been posted and wonder how these Kool-Aid drinkers can sit here and believe it all. I interviewed Mark Eglinton, and he said through the in-depth interviews that he was doing with John he concluded that John was an atheist, he didn't believe in God or any particular creator, at least from my understanding.

So, if you're going into a Telegram group and you're seeing all this pro-Christian rhetoric — even though I'm in that, I follow the teachings of Jesus — that's not John McAfee talking about God. It's crazy

WHACKD – By the time of your third interview, John was in Cuba. What comes to mind from that time?

RiceTVx – One interesting thing that happened in Cuba was that someone in the Cuban government or military had a meeting with John and they gave him a heads-up to the fact that the United States was wanting the Cubans to hold him for extradition. The Cubans gave John time to disappear so that they didn't have to hold him for extradition. John was a big fan of Cuba. There's all this negative talk about what Cuba is like and he gave a real perspective as to how the media falsely reports a lot of things. At the time the US media were reporting that the Cuban people were so hungry they were eating rats and stuff like that, John made a point of showing it wasn't like that. He showed that the Cubans he was dealing with were fine people.

Before John and Janice went off-grid they were very transparent with me about everything that I asked. Once they made it to the UK and went off-grid they wouldn't tell me anything. All they could tell me was to provide the days and times I was available, then they'll let me know what works. After my fourth interview with him, he was in the Faraday cage.

I was going to be attending a conference in Philadelphia. It was kind of a fork of the Anarchapulco conference that Jeff Berwick, Dollar Vigilante, puts on. They were doing it in Philadelphia and it was called Anarchadelphia. I had asked John if he would record a speech for that conference, for the anarchists, kind of give a personalised message, and he agreed to do it.

He recorded it for me, sent me the file, and never asked me for anything to do it. That was one of my favourite memories of John because as you might know, John got in trouble with the SEC because he would do paid endorsements and not disclose about it. So, he was getting paid a lot to do those kinds of videos. He would have demanded a lot of money for that, but he did it for me, for free, which was a blessing.

In that third interview I did with John whilst he was in Cuba, he said "There's a reason why I do so many interviews with you" and that he wouldn't ever tell me no, even telling people to make sure that they're subscribed to my channel. Those kinds of things are priceless in my relationship with him.

WHACKD – Around that time, John said his body double and multiple international campaign managers were hospitalised and possibly poisoned. Do you have any more information about that period?

RiceTVx – Well, I believe it to be true. John had several different clone-type, body-double people. I mean, they weren't clones, but they looked similar to John, if not just like him. I never knew any of these individuals. Some names were given to me in the past. I'm sure if I dig up through my notes, I'd be able to figure out some of these people, but for the sake of John's safety, I didn't have a lot of personal information about these individuals because it would kind of take away from the purpose of having them.

Everybody knew John had 'representatives,' but I can say that every time that I interviewed John it was the real John that I interviewed. Even talking to Janice about her having to identify his body, she says that it was definitely John and not any of the individuals in question.

WHACKD – When John arrived in the Dominican Republic, what events led to his arrest and his subsequent release?

RiceTVx – He wasn't there for very long and as soon as he got there, he was pretty much in custody. Apparently, it had something to do with calls about drugs and firearms on their ship when they were going from international waters into the Dominican Republic territory. What's customary out there, in that situation, is you take everything you have and put it out in the open, so the authorities can see that you're not concealing anything. Janice told me a story which wasn't included in the interview that we published. It's something that we do plan on doing a follow-up interview and answering a little bit better, I can give you the short story version of what I understand.

John was going to be deported back to Cuba by the Dominican Republic to then be extradited to the US. Because John was born in the UK, a lot of people don't know that, but John was a dual citizen, and as a dual citizen he legally had the right to demand deportation back to the UK, but the authorities were trying to deny that.

So, let me set the stage for this. John liked to mess with people, almost in a childish kind of way, he found a lot of satisfaction in it. It was one of his pastimes, to just really fuck with people and get one over on them, in a funny way. So, he faked a heart attack and was taken to the hospital. Had he not faked the heart attack, they were going to try to extradite him to the United States. So, this was a delay tactic, John faking that heart attack and going to the hospital gave just enough time for his attorney to arrive in the Dominican Republic directly. Based on what I'm remembering Janice telling me, the lawyer was telling John "What you did worked, but you can't recover too fast." It would have looked obvious what he did. I found that amusing, how he plays these childish pranks on people, and on the inside, he's laughing his hysterical laughs that everyone is familiar with.

WHACKD – There was also the joke of "Well, that won't work a third time." He did the same thing in Guatemala in 2012, so that time was the second time he faked a health emergency to outwit the authorities.

RiceTVx – Janice has shared with me a couple of other little stories of where he's done things that are equally as childish or prankish, just not on such a large scale. I asked Janice how she and John had met because there were a lot of rumours that Janice was hired to kill John, as she's a former prostitute and all that stuff. Well, she told me that when they first met it was the day that he had arrived in Miami after John's Belize saga. Janice randomly ran into him; he figured out she was a prostitute and she ultimately convinced him to spend some time with her.

She said that when they went to the room John was, if you can imagine him, standing on his tip-toes and kind of going up and down, his hands kind of together with a maniacal kind of laugh going on. She asked him what that was about, and he was like "Well, this might be a weird request, but would you mind if you just hold me for a little while." She was cool with it, so he got excited about that. Then when he was like laying on the bed with her in some fashion. I don't know exactly how it took place, but he fell asleep.

It was just the whole idea of his kind of like being like an excited child, wanting to spend some intimate time with somebody, not in a sexual manner necessarily, but just to get some kind of human closeness. From my understanding, the way the story was explained to me, Janice was expecting them to get naked and her to do her job. He wasn't wanting that, and I think he also surprised her by being like 'Hey, you probably thought I was gonna be like everyone else, just here to get what I paid for, but I just want to cuddle." I'm sure that's not as exciting as faking a heart attack but it still has its equally childish play elements that I mentioned earlier.

WHACKD – Your next interview with John was on the ninth of August 2019, the day before Jeffrey Epstein was Whackd. John was now recording from his Faraday cage room in an undisclosed location somewhere in Europe. What are your thoughts on that time?

RiceTVx – I was really worried about John, all that time on the run just hiding from everybody, at his age and stuff. How was it going to have its effect on him, you know, that's a lot of it.

WHACKD – Your next interview was with John and Adam Kokesh, who was also running for president in the Libertarian Party. Can you speak about that interview?

RiceTVx – I suggested to them multiple times that they team up. I think I even said it back in the fifth interview that we did. Ultimately, they decided to go ahead and team up. Adam's press secretary Marcus Pulis and Janice made sure that I was going to get the first interview with the two of them together, which I think ended up being the only interview with the two of them, like that at least, so that was cool. It was a different kind of interview from the others; it wasn't me asking about what he had going on, and we weren't talking about current events or being on the run. It was like sitting in on a meeting that I wasn't supposed to be a part of.

It was the first time that they had gotten together and spoken since they had agreed to run for president together. They were 'Team End the Fed,' that's what I named them, or maybe they named it that. So, Team End the Fed had a presidential and vice-presidential meeting with me, Chris Rice, just eavesdropping in, recording it for my YouTube channel and calling it an interview.

One crazy thing, though, the interview that I suggested that Adam and John team up in, ended up being my sixth interview with both of them. So, I interviewed both of them five times separately, and then the sixth interview with both of them huddled together on screen, which was a cool experience.

WHACKD – Was John able to participate much in any presidential debates during that period in 2020?

RiceTVx – He did, very minimally, but it wasn't a lot. I didn't have the opportunity to check out a lot of his stuff and I don't know what's still available on the internet.

I remember one of the things that were mentioned in the sixth interview, the one where I was eavesdropping in their meeting, was them talking about appearing, how and where they were going to be debating, and stuff to that effect. John did do stuff like that but at the same time the party didn't take John very seriously, so he wasn't invited and included in the reindeer games. There were also smaller little things that weren't necessarily put on by The Libertarian Party. I know that John did get involved in some of those and made appearances, just how many, I don't know.

WHACKD – During your next interview with John on March 18, 2020, the pandemic had just been declared. With the new coronavirus restrictions in place, both John and Janice were in lockdown in Spain. Do you have any insights or stories from that time?

RiceTVx – To me, that was one of my favourite interviews with John. He was very public about everything that was going on with him whilst on the run and everything that I had as far as questions for the most part had already been answered. So, at that point, the interview was more about asking him questions about time travel, and psychedelics. I even asked him about Q-Anon and extra-terrestrials.

It was kind of an oddball interview. I was asking him like "What is the typical day for John McAfee?" You know, just questions that had nothing to do with being on the run because he couldn't say where he was. He was limited with all that information. We pretty much knew everything, so it was redundant to just kind of keep going over it and I wanted something a little bit more special with that.

WHACKD – After the 'End the Fed' interview, in September, John celebrated his 75th birthday in Spain. However, by October

2021 he was arrested on charges of tax evasion. How did you hear about this? What were your thoughts on the situation?

RiceTVx – As far as him being arrested, I found that out like almost everyone else: on Twitter. When I found out, it sucked. You know, not just from a selfish perspective, but am I ever going to be able to talk to John again? John was just a good dude. I had the same feelings that John had. If he was going to be arrested then he probably wasn't going to see the light of day, so many people wanted to take him out.

Now, another thing that didn't happen that I wish I had taken advantage of, in June of 2021 there was a Shitcoin conference going on by Kenn Bosak. Sometime in late April or May 2021, I talked with Janice about interviewing John. I assumed that he had a phone in prison, so I asked If there was any way to do like a short interview. I was told, "There's no way he could talk on the phone to do a phone interview."

Janice said that she talked to John and he said that if I would write out some questions, he would have either written the answers back, or he would have told Janice what to write down. We also agreed that I was going to release that interview as an NFT. A couple of weeks later I had to get prepared for going out of town to go to Bitcoin 21 and the Shitcoin Conference 2021. When I have to go out of town, I usually get ahead work-wise, so I have videos coming out whilst I'm out of town. So, I go into work mode and I'm crunching through it all. The next thing I know, June 23rd comes around and the news of John's death broke. I never had a chance to put together the questions and send them to him to get that interview done. So, I have a few regrets with John, not getting that handwritten interview, and then not going to go visit him in person.

WHACKD – Did you have any other kind of communication with him whilst he was incarcerated?

RiceTVx – I didn't have any kind of direct communication with him while he was in prison. Also unbeknownst to me, John didn't have a phone in prison, so he couldn't be tweeting. He talked to Janice three times a day and they talked the maximum amount of time allowed, which I think was either 15 or 20 minutes each time. So, if I'm not mistaken, all the communication that took place on John's Twitter account since the time of his arrest was all him communicating through Janice. There may have been another individual involved with transcribing information and posting it, but as far as I know, it was directly John to Janice to Twitter. That might explain a little bit of difference in some of the ways things were said.

In the interview with Janice, I had to ask Janice very specifically "Was John suicidal?" You know, he was 75 years old. He had to go up and down stairs, which wasn't the easiest thing for him. There were some things where he was dealing with physical pain whereas before he might have been drinking, even taking ibuprofen or aspirin or something, just to alleviate some of those old age pains. He was dealing with all that kind of stuff in prison.

I could imagine after a couple of months his body started to have to deal with it all naturally. The depression of sitting in jail until you're extradited, what's going to happen to you when you get extradited. Even though he felt like something could happen to him in prison, he didn't feel like the SEC and IRS charges were going to keep him in prison for the rest of his life. Whether something was to happen to him while he was in prison was a different story, but he wasn't suicidal in the manner of the kind of situation where there is no light at the end of the tunnel.

I question what happened with John. I question everything because you just can't know. While I'm talking to Janice and interviewing Janice; John could be in the next room for all I know. No, dealing with the pain that I see in her eyes and things like that, and the emotion that I feel from her, I don't feel like that is the case.

WHACKD – Are you able to speak about Janice's current situation at the moment?

RiceTVx – From what I understand after talking to Mark Eglinton, I don't want to speak ill of the dead, but it didn't appear that John had very much money left at the time of his arrest, or whilst on the run. It doesn't seem like Janice is well off in any fashion. I don't think she has access to any of his cryptocurrency. The fact that his body hasn't been released just brings off all these fucking "I don't know" and "What ifs." You can look at it from the most logical side and still say the Spanish authorities are covering something up.

The whole thing is just shitty, from a human rights standpoint, in not releasing his body. It's nothing to do with John or who he is, as a human being, a fellow brother, a part of our species who deserves the same respect that all of us deserve. I've never heard of a situation where somebody has been held after their death for over a year.

Another thing that bothered me about this whole thing was the media and the way that they spun all this, talking about John committing suicide and saying he hanged himself. After doing the interview with Janice and learning more in-depth about the situation, when the correctional officers, the jailers, whatever they're called in Spain, discovered John he wasn't dead, and then he died.

They tried to revive him. So, if what they're saying took place, took place, and there was no foul play or anything like that, then they should say that John died of complications from attempted suicide. If they didn't find him dead with a noose or sheet around his neck, then how can they say he committed suicide? Then when there's no official autopsy, no official death certificate, no official cause of death, how can Wikipedia and all these different institutions with websites, newspaper articles, and all the media corporations, how can they say that John committed suicide, if, in fact, that wasn't the case at all. Either way, whichever you look at it, he didn't kill himself, because he wasn't found dead. So that's one of the things that bothers me about all that. Or, did John pay somebody to get out? You know, because that's the only other thing: the corruption of the Spanish authorities. Did somebody get paid to help John getaway? Is that why they can't release anything?

I suggested the change.org petition to Janice just because of the semi-successes that FreeRoss had using the site. I think that they got over half a million signatures which was enough to bring into question whether or not the President would grant clemency, so it brought that kind of attention to it. I've suggested to Janice, and this is just kind of keeping the legacy of John alive, that when she gets back to the States, she should start making appearances at conferences. I'd like to connect her up with Lynn Albrecht, Ross Albrecht's mom from the Silk Road stuff, as she's going around to conferences trying to bring attention to bring clemency to reduce his sentence because, at this point, her son is never going to get out of prison. To me, John and Ross are two of the biggest Renegades for crypto so it makes sense to have the two family members of each standing up together.

But I mean, that stuff's not gonna be until later. Janice has no inclination, no plans, and no desire to leave Spain until John's body is released. She missed one of her kids' graduation a couple of months ago, and proms. There are things that she has been missing out on as a mother because she feels she can't leave Spain. She feels like she needs to be there and I get it. At the same time, she is always looking around her shoulders, like, she's always worried that something's going to happen to her.

On another note, unless I'm not being given the complete truth of things, and that's possible, it doesn't seem like John left anything for Janice. There wasn't even an attorney situation set up, there wasn't anything, sometimes you'll have it set up where you'll pay for your burial and then you give all the information to your attorney and upon your death, the attorney makes sure they execute it. There wasn't any of that: no foundation, none of the things that people who are wealthy and important do. None of that stuff was even done.

It makes me question John's mentality toward things. Janice told me that there was no post-mortem attorney to deal with John's death or his estate, like what the fuck? Even if he didn't own very much property there still should have been something in place. I've had to question some of his madness.

WHACKD – During the time that you've known John, did he change your outlook or perspective in any particular way? If so, how?

RiceTVx – Well, it's kind of a weird way of looking at things, I'm not saying that I am John McAfee, but I can see a lot of myself in him. Seeing John as an older guy gives me hope for myself as an older guy. I felt a lot of kinship with the two of us and I think that's one of the reasons why we got along so well and he liked me as an interviewer. Maybe he saw a part of himself in me like I saw a part of myself in him?

It gave me hope, too, because when I think of older people, I think of people who just retire, they only want to be content, and they're not trying to do anything to change the world as they've already paid their dues. As old as John was, he was continuing to do his thing and not just be like some grandpa sitting at home unconcerned with the rest of the world. It gave me a lot of inspiration and hope for my own future, as selfish as that might sound.

It's better to do what makes you happy. I could tell John was doing what made him happy. That's the other important thing to take away from all this: even though John was on the run and taking a stand for all this time, he still enjoyed his life.

John was very in touch, but he was an enigma.

Chapter Five
Adam Kokesh

WHACKD – Hi Adam, thank you for doing this. When did you first become aware of John McAfee?

Adam Kokesh – Well, I've been a fan of John McAfee for a long time, I realised that the pain in the ass that McAfee Antivirus had become was not as a result of his genius, but the result of him leaving and selling out from the company. That first made me wonder about his life, then follow his story a little bit. Going to Belize, evading the authorities, and the other fun stuff he was doing there, it was all very exciting.

I didn't have any personal connection at the time so I wasn't compelled to get into it, tease it apart, or make any kind of judgement about it for myself. I got to know John as a fan from a distance when he ran for the Libertarian Party nomination for president in 2016.

Specifically, I remember him telling a story in one of the debates about getting caught walking down the street, smoking a joint, getting taken to jail, getting released, then going right back and smoking a joint in the same place, getting arrested again, going right back to jail to go do the same all over again. I took that story to heart and it was humbling for someone like me who is known for being a civil disobedience activist and for him to be like "You step over lines, huh, I don't even see lines." I was like, God dammit, I want to be John McAfee when I grow up.

WHACKD – What events led up to you being involved with John McAfee?

Adam Kokesh – When I was running in the U.S Presidential race in 2020, John was evading the authorities and I got to run alongside him. He made an announcement offering all the candidates to be his running mate and we all turned him down but I must have missed the memo and I was like "Fuck no, I would love to have John McAfee as my running mate. That's fucking insane." I was a credible top-tier candidate contender and he said "All right, yeah, I'll be Adam's running mate."

It was a little confusing strategy wise but it was cool for me to say John McAfee is my running mate and that we're going to work together, with me in the United States and him wherever the heck he is. It was an exciting offer. What we represented, the two of us together for the Libertarian Party in 2020, of course, was too good for all the corrupt forces to let us win the nomination.

WHACKD – Did you get the opportunity to appear in any debates with John during that time?

Adam Kokesh – Sadly no, but John was debating in 2016. I was in Vegas and I endorsed him in a little selfie video in 2020. He was abroad so he wasn't able to participate in any of the debates that I did as a candidate. So, when he was my running mate we weren't debating in any format, but it would have been fun. I wish even virtually for us to have shared the same stage sort of debating against each other or as a team.

WHACKD – You asked John to read your book 'Freedom' and John later endorsed it on Facebook, do you think reading that book had any influence on John's 2016 campaign?

Adam Kokesh – Oh, absolutely. A huge part of my relationship with John was that I was his libertarian influence, in part through my book 'Freedom.' When he was running for the presidential nomination in 2016, around the beginning of that campaign, he was talking about Cyber Security for America. I was like "God dammit, he wants the government to do cybersecurity." I'm not doubting his credentials at all, or his intentions, but holy shit, John, the kind of genius you are wanting to do it with the government, it made me not want to support him at first because he was taking the pro-government security position. While he was extremely libertarian in spirit; it wasn't a great start policy-wise.

In 2016 someone convinced him to get a 'party insider' type to be his running mate so he got Judd Weiss, who is a close friend of mine. Judd then asked me to endorse John so I said I'll endorse John if he reads my book and shows that he has at least acknowledged the libertarian philosophical perspective. He read it and I noticed right away in the policy positions that he had taken it all to heart. Instead of saying "I'm a cybersecurity expert therefore you [the Government] should trust me with American cybersecurity, as your president" he started saying "Because of my cybersecurity expertise, I see that we need to get the government completely out of this entirely," and that was a major shift. It gave me the confidence to support him in 2016 and it's one of the greatest honours of my life to have had that influence on him.

WHACKD – Other than your libertarian values what else did you and John share in common?

Adam Kokesh – Well, something that John McAfee and I had in common, is we both liked buying drugs and giving them away. One different thing though is that I liked the healthier drugs like cannabis, psilocybin, LSD, and drugs that offer therapeutic enlightening, whereas John preferred other recreational drugs too. In some ways, I like to think of myself as an evolution of John McAfee but without the same technological keenness. I've said before hacking politics is civil disobedience, living by principles, being self-sustainable, and tax avoidance and I feel very humbled by it all. I understand that my impact is probably a fraction of John McAfee's but in some ways, my goal in life is to live up to John McAfee's standard.

WHACKD – How did you and John fare as a team in the 2020 presidential run?

Adam Kokesh – Well, to answer that question, I'll take a break for a bong rip. During the time that John and I were running mates, we never got to meet in person. We met in person on other occasions, but during the time that we were running mates we never actually met in person, or again after that. But it was a surreal experience. I had met him in person a few times where we hung out, but we spent a lot more time together in joint interviews, strategy meetings or going over things as running mates. So, did we make a good team? Yes, in that context, but it wasn't particularly challenging to be running mates in the libertarian primary and coordinate everything we needed to do for that. His wife Janice was very helpful during that time and John also had some good people around him who took the campaign seriously enough, while saving him from getting murdered while getting his message out and calling attention to his platform.

I think the potential that we had as a team, in terms of what we represented, our résumés, personality-wise, and our unique types of credibility, we represented an incredible team and an incredible potential for a message that got a lot of people excited in the Libertarian Party. It was really unfortunate that the LP primaries had a lot of corruption and a lot of manipulation, and because 2020 was done virtually, it was a very weird time. All the corruption with COVID, and as is always the case in politics, surprise, surprise, there was a lot of manipulation and rarely do the best candidates ever win.

WHACKD – I noticed you read 'No Domain: The John McAfee Tapes' by Mark Eglinton. What did you take away from reading the book?

Adam Kokesh – I mean, there's so much that absorbs John MacAfee's spirit. I don't want to say it's my favourite but the first part that comes to mind, something I hadn't fully appreciated before was the many applications of his talents in his early tech career, pre–McAfee Antivirus, where he was able to be the guy who goes in once a week to work for a few hours and provide so much value that he's still basically running shit and making more money than any one man needs. It's inspiring in a way that I don't think a lot of people are capable of really absorbing. He's like some kind of freak genius who found his perfect amusements and I think if everybody were in touch with their genius, and their capabilities, they could each strive to have the same level of impact.

WHACKD – After nearly two years on the run John was then imprisoned in October 2020. What was your reaction to this?

Adam Kokesh – My main response to John getting locked up was disappointment in John. He got sloppy and got caught. I don't want to say he should have been smarter because I don't think it was stupidity, but he should have been more careful or more deliberately evasive. I don't want to say he would have been alive today, but he might have still been one step ahead of them.

WHACKD – On several occasions, John claimed to have a Dead Man's Switch whereby 31 terabytes of incriminating data would be released. Do you have any thoughts on that?

Adam Kokesh – I do not claim to have an insight into John's strategic thinking and I don't want to put odds on it. I will say that if I was in the position to make that bluff to protect my life and be credible with that bluff and for it to have some deterrent effect, I would do it. If it was real as he described, perhaps once he was locked up, they were able to secure data or they were able to find who had a copy of that data or the keys to it or whatever and then take them out. Then they could take McAfee out and know that the data dump isn't coming. It could be either of those possibilities, I really don't pretend to know.

WHACKD – Who do you think had the greatest motive to silence John?

Adam Kokesh – I don't think there was one singular malicious conspiracy against John. I think it was more a network of loosely described conspiracies, quote, unquote, within various government agencies. If he had evaded them and stayed quiet, they would have let him live, but he got caught and once the charges were out there, he was ripe to get caught, and he got caught. He was still in a jail cell making noise and they said 'We can't let him go because he will make more noise, and we can't bring him back to the United States on trial because he will make WAY more noise.'

That would wake people up, it would fuck with their whole taxation racket so at some point someone made that decision, since he's here, and he's still making noise, well we're just going to kill him. That's what's going on.

WHACKD – Do you believe John's death was somebody setting an example?

Adam Kokesh – Yeah, they don't want you to fall for the lie, they want you to accept it as a threat. I just want to say for myself, I joined the Marine Corps and I'm a decorated combat veteran. There are all sorts of stuff I could be doing with life and I've decided to live a relatively modest life, because of the constraints of liability that comes with certain kinds of wealth. John McAfee made something like 100 million dollars and who knows how much more selling out his share of McAfee associates and you know, other deals that he was involved with. He got a lot of money on paper and that was an excuse for the government to fuck with him. I don't ever want that kind of money.

WHACKD – What are your thoughts on the alleged suicide note that was released after John's death?

Adam Kokesh – Yeah, bullshit. It's like thinking about how much we've been lied to with COVID, the lies are not even credible anymore, and the narrative has just absolutely crumbled, but it isn't about getting you to believe the lies, it's to get you to accept them. I think that that's the real point. That's where we're at with these great modern first-world governments: they don't care if you know that they're lying.

It's like Solzhenitsyn said: "We know they're lying and they know that we know they're lying, but they keep lying." The point is not to trick you into believing a lie, the point is to bully you into accepting it, and then they can get you to go along with anything. That's the kind of power that governments have taken on right now.

WHACKD – John's body has been in a morgue since his death, why do you think it's taking so long to release his body?

Adam Kokesh – Well I would hardly say that it's worthy of wonder, it should be pretty obvious. There's a larger effort to obfuscate the circumstances of his death, and of course, prevent an independent autopsy, or release of the body for any analysis beyond the official one that backs up their obvious bullshit suicide narrative. People need to know it's certainly more political than anything.

John McAfee is still sending us a message whilst in that box in Spain. His lifestyle, what he represents, and his message have such power that it still has to be locked up. It can't even be allowed out long enough to be buried or burned, it has to be secluded in a metal box and forgotten.

WHACKD – If John was still here, what message would he have for people?

Adam Kokesh – I think I could sum up the message of John McAfee's life and ethos into two words: become ungovernable.

Chapter Six
Peter Galanko (XVG Whale)

WHACKD – Hi, thank you for doing this Peter.

XVG Whale – First off, I want to start by saying all due respect and condolences to Janice McAfee. I can't imagine what she is going through. I was at their house for six days and she was a great host. Janice kept to herself mostly but she was very polite. I didn't really connect directly with her as much as I did with John, but I did go for sushi and to the movies with her, John, and their security team. So, I don't want to be disrespectful in the circumstances but at the same time I didn't necessarily have a completely great experience with McAfee, so I'm just wanting to be straight up about that, and I do want to be respectful of Janice.

WHACKD – Understood. Can you introduce yourself, and describe how you first entered the world of John McAfee?

XVG Whale – Well, my name is Peter Galanko, in 2017 I went by the moniker 'XVG Whale' (@XVGwhale on Twitter). That account was later hacked and suspended and that may have had something to do with the dispute I had with John. As for how I became involved in the world of McAfee, there are people in the cryptocurrency community that are known as Verge Fam and we were trying to get McAfee's attention by tweeting at him. I wasn't closely following McAfee then, but I saw their tweets and even got a follow back from John, which meant I could DM him. There was also Verge Tip Bot that no longer exists. It was shut down in 2018, and it was used to send tips through Twitter. Someone had sent a tip to McAfee in XVG and he replied to it and retweeted it. I wasn't sure if that was an endorsement of XVG as I had previously sent him a DM about a week before. So, I DM'd him again and I was like "How about doing an interview?" and so he responded to me with an invite to visit. "Let's do an hour or two interview, come to my address here," and I was like "All right, sure, I'll drive over there."

I drove from Ohio to Tennessee where McAfee was living. Initially, it was just supposed to be an interview rather than staying at his house for multiple nights. McAfee did a lot of interviews and he had his security around him but John didn't often have a lot of people to stay at his home like that, so I did get a little bit of a unique perspective on his daily life.

WHACKD – What was your first impression when you arrived?

XVG Whale – Well, McAfee played a bit of a game with me when I arrived, the door opened and John was like "Who are you?" I was like "XVG Whale from Twitter, you told me to come over?" He's like "I don't know what you're talking about." He was just fucking with me, then he let me in. So, at first, he pretended to not know who I was, as a joke, and then he brought me into the house.

My initial plan was to interview for my YouTube channel but we got talking. He asked me about my background, about cryptocurrency, what I've been doing and that sort of stuff but we weren't recording at that time. Then he offered drinks and there was plenty of weed around. I brought some of my own too. We started smoking and drinking and he was like "Well, if you guys are smoking and drinking, you can't drive now, you might as well spend the night. There's an extra room right here." So, I was like "All right, sure, I'll spend the night." So that was my initial interaction with John McAfee.

WHACKD – What was waking up at McAfee's like?

XVG Whale – I remember one morning, there was a bathroom next to our bedroom and it was connected to the kitchen. So, I got up, went to the bathroom and found McAfee with his security in the kitchen pouring up shot glasses of tequila. McAfee was like "Hey, good morning, Peter. Want to have a shot of tequila?" So, I had some shots of tequila first thing in the morning. On the first morning, though, John had baked eggs, and they were pretty good. He used some sort of curry spices and stuff. So, McAfee made breakfast that first morning.

WHACKD – Other than tequila and eggs, how else did you spend the week?

XVG Whale – There was a lot of talk about crypto, there was a lot of drinking and a lot of conversations. McAfee would tell his war stories about Belize and Guatemala multiple times, and he would often be doing business calls with some important people or talking in interviews. He was supposed to do another interview the week that I was there. We were going to get a limo and I was going to join him, not to be included in the interview, but just to join him. It was for some news station but it got cancelled because Alex (John's security guard) had a doctor's appointment and McAfee didn't feel comfortable without the security.

So, there was a lot of drinking, McAfee would drink about a litre and a half of liquor a day. One of his security guards was nicknamed 'Shaky' because his hands would always be shaking. I don't know if that was from drugs or drinking so much all the time.

WHACKD – Did you get up to anything else notable whilst you were there?

XVG Whale – One interesting experience I had was shooting a silenced sniper rifle right off John's front porch. It was a big yard and his security would shoot critters like raccoons and other stuff because they had a lot of dogs and when the dogs would start barking, everyone would have their guns drawn in case there was something about to happen. So, if they saw raccoons or skunks they would shoot them. So, I was out there, we were just shooting Coke cans and I impressed Alex. My first shot was like 100 feet away where I hit the can on the first try. Then Alex was standing on the porch shooting and at first, we were just targeting and practising with cans and then a raccoon came up, Alex shot it once or twice then handed me the gun, so I did the kill shot. It was a pretty nice neighbourhood, I don't think we're supposed to be doing that there, but we did.

WHACKD – Do you recall other funny moments from your stay?

XVG Whale – Yeah, one funny story. I was drunk one night when I was at McAfee's and I accidentally knocked over a bowl next to me, it scared all the security guards and they pulled out their guns. I was so drunk and high that I just started laughing. I wasn't scared of any threats when I was there and I didn't expect to stay so many nights, but John would put his hand on my shoulder and it'd be like "Peter, why don't you stay another night?" My girlfriend did start to feel a little like she was being held hostage though.

WHACKD – Did you see any interesting features in John's home that stood out to you?

XVG Whale – Yeah, one interesting thing is that McAfee's room was on the other side of the house from where I was staying and he had a metal security door that was bolted shut. He was constantly worried about being raided or some home invasion so he had a bolted-shut metal door and he spent a lot of time in that part of the house. I never really saw that part of the house. I saw the rest of the house besides that part. Some of the security would live in a bedroom down in the basement. It was a two-floor house, with a bedroom in the basement. Then John's cousin, I think it was his biological cousin, was a former detective and he came to visit three or four days after I got there. He was moved into the room that my girlfriend and I were staying in, so we went to another guestroom upstairs. We stayed in two different rooms throughout this thing.

WHACKD – In 2017 it was reported that John went on a naked shooting spree throughout that Tennessee home. Did you see any apparent signs of this when you visited?

XVG Whale – That shooting spree happened about two weeks before he invited me to his home. I have wondered if one reason he wanted a guest there, right next to the back porch and the garage, two possible entrances to the house, was I like a canary in the coal mine? But, as far as the shooting spree goes, he did show me a hole in the floor. Next to the bar is a kitchen and that is the only bullet hole that I saw, in the article it mentioned him shooting into the ceiling. But I saw no gunshots in the ceiling.

When I was there, he asked me to come outside with him and he had two cans of bear spray to spray under the back porch. We sprayed all this bear spray under the back porch and he said he was doing that so people wouldn't crawl under the porch and hide. I thought it was probably to keep the raccoons and skunks away so they don't spook the dogs. He felt threatened when the dogs would bark, and they would all have their guns drawn instantly. He thought cartel people were after him, and he told stories that he hid under cars and that sort of thing. He had a lot of stories like that. Sometimes I wonder how much of it were stories told for publicity, or paranoia, or how much of it was real.

WHACKD – Did John share any stories about himself regarding his time in Belize?

XVG Whale – Yeah, McAfee gave me his rendition. I haven't watched the documentaries but I've read some articles online. I'm not sure how much the story that he gave me differs from what's published out there. John's rendition is that he moved to Belize and because he was well known as a wealthy person the Belizean government were trying to put pressure on him for endorsement donations. At first, I think he paid them but they came back and they wanted more. Instead of paying more, John offered to give them a whole bunch of computers from his former business. According to John, all those computers had spyware on them, which is how he collected the alleged intel implicating people in Belize, people in the cartel and the US government.

The other thing that he mentioned is that he was doing medical research to develop some sort of medication in the jungle of Belize, but others have said that he was just doing a meth lab out there. I don't know. I wasn't there. I'm sure his version is that he was doing legitimate medical research in the jungle. Let's just say that the product was real and he was doing legitimate business there because that's the version able to be seen, but I don't know about any of that stuff.

After that happened, you probably know most of the story, he got out of Belize and then got to Guatemala where he was arrested. John agreed to do a Vice News interview and they posted a picture that had his geolocation tag in the metadata, so that's how they found him.

John's version of the story is that he hit it off great with the prison guards, they had him out of his cell, he helped run the prison, and he was giving them advice and working directly with the prison guards so he said he was treated well. He also had an expensive estate that was burned down. Not much was stolen but he had a lot of expensive paintings and sunken mahogany, which is mahogany that has been semi-fossilised at the bottom of the Mississippi River and brought back up. That place was destroyed. While that was happening, he was granted to be able to come back to the United States. He told me he had no money left when he got back to the US. A friend spotted him $5,000 and he spent that $5,000 on Janice.

WHACKD – How long after your visit was it that your relationship with John started to sour?

XVG Whale – So, all I knew was McAfee was big in the crypto space and that he gave interviews, so I tried making some network connections. After I left McAfee's house he was like "What about some endorsement money to endorse XVG?" I was like "I don't have money like that right now. Thanks, but no thanks," sort of thing. I had known that McAfee celebrated his then recent birthday with Jihan Wu and Roger Ver in Hong Kong and I wanted to get connected with Jihan Wu.

When McAfee and I were drunk at his house, I was like "My girlfriend has a business trip in Hong Kong, if I go with her could you connect me with Jihan Wu? Do you think I can meet him?" McAfee was like "Sure, absolutely." When I went to Hong Kong, I called McAfee, and he answered his phone. I don't know if he remembered that conversation but he wasn't able to help me, but he would follow up with me about the money. He knew Jihan Wu, and I had a lot of people asking me about mining rigs. I was like "John if you can help me get a direct order through Bitmain even at retail prices, I have people that will lock in $3 million of purchase orders right now, I can get you paid 250 grand and I can pay you in XVG as a business deal cut rather than an endorsement." Bitcoin was skyrocketing and it was impossible to connect directly with Bitmain at the time. John was direct with the owner of Bitmain and I wasn't looking to pay for an endorsement. So, after that, I received texts from a different number that mentioned multiple things I and John had discussed on the phone, so I knew it was McAfee's number.

So, we're texting and he's pressing me to pay him for an endorsement. I'm not part of the Verge currency core team. It's not a pre-mine. It's a community thing. But I was like, look, I'm going to meet with the developer and founder of Verge in Florida, I'm going to talk to him about it, and maybe we can work something out. So, he went ahead and endorsed XVG, which was right around the end of 2017, by posting about it on Instagram. I wasn't using Instagram so I didn't see that stuff, but I had screenshots. Then, Verge hit an all-time high and it was a perfect combination of factors: we had this McAfee endorsement, the Wraith protocol release, and I had been helping to grow the Verge community on Twitter giving out tips and during contests. For people that used the Verge Fam hashtag at the time, I would send them tips with the Verge tip bot. I sent hundreds and hundreds of dollars to random people; Twitter was buzzing and Verge was mooning.

Then I met with Justin Vendetta and I got a text from McAfee's secondary number, he wanted a million dollars. I'm like "Yeah, can't do a million dollars." He got super pissed off and said "Give me $100,000 in an hour and never talk to me again." I just ignored him. Then he said that he was going to send me to jail, it was pretty threatening. After that, I got threatening text messages from random numbers that couldn't be traced. My XVG Gmail account was hacked, $5,000 in XVG was taken out of my Twitter tip bot, and I lost my Twitter account at 60,000 followers. I was on the come-up, and my stuff was hacked. Twitter wouldn't help me out either. I wondered if McAfee had connections at Twitter because Twitter's customer service wouldn't help me out with the hack. It felt like it was a payola gatekeeper sort of thing where it's like "Oh, you want to be a crypto influencer, you've got to pay your fee." So, I had mixed feelings about McAfee. At the time, one of his security guards was like "Don't worry about it. He's like a barking chihuahua, all bark and no bite."

WHACKD – Who did you hear that from in John's security?

XVG Whale – He was a vet with PTSD. I kind of feel bad for him because he was fired for falling asleep on the night shift. He was really chill. He would make Canna-butter and stuff like that. He was sort of like a hippie vet. Two years ago, though, he was arrested in Florida for breaking into a courtroom and sitting in the judge's chair with a sickle on some psychotic break. It was published in the news at the time.

Anyway, I was in contact with him when all this was going on and he was saying not to worry. At that time, I was staying with my girlfriend at her family's house and I was in the basement of my girlfriend's family home; they're gun friendly. We had a plan in case he sent some goons, like, we go to the basement and have guns ready to shoot upwards in case somebody tried to come down. That wasn't what I was looking for when I went to his house.

WHACKD – So, John felt he was owed for an endorsement he made?

XVG Whale – Yeah, I mentioned in text messages to him that the SEC had made a law where paid endorsements must be disclosed and he made the endorsement before I made any arrangements for a paid endorsement, there was no deal made. He jumped the gun and did the endorsement early then applied pressure to pay him afterwards, which if I did pay him, would be an undisclosed paid endorsement.

After that, I was looking to do business with him in mining rig sales to pay him legitimately, then he started withdrawing his endorsement of Verge. He said "My power to destroy is far stronger than my power to build," basically saying he's going to ruin Verge.

Eventually, he did Ghost by McAfee which I think was slightly inspired by Verges Wraith Protocol but he did that a few years later. He was also telling me when I was at his house that because he sold McAfee Antivirus, he had also sold rights to use his name 'McAfee' for software. He wasn't sure if he was going to be able to release the coin using his name but I guess he got that sorted out a few years later. Originally, he planned to release the coin in 2018. He wanted me to be a project manager or social media manager for that and John invited me to move into the house right next door in Tennessee. I was going to visit him again in January to sort things out to be like an assistant type of thing working directly with him, but then we had the falling out so I never moved out there. I think McAfee wanted instant gratification and I think because of his drinking when on a bender, he had mood changes quickly.

WHACKD – After you met John, you were visited by the FBI. Are you able to speak on those interactions?

XVG Whale – Yeah, so about a year and a half after I visited John the FBI started their investigation probe into McAfee and came to speak to me. It was not a good morning. I've got an autoimmune disease and at that time I was starting to feel sick. I didn't know that I had the disease at that time. I had gotten drunk the night before so I was hungover as shit too. I get a knock on the door, it's six o'clock in the morning. I'm not a morning person, and it's an FBI badge. I'm like "What the fuck." Fortunately, it wasn't as bad as I thought. They investigated me but didn't have anything on me. There was also someone impersonating me as XVG Whale on Reddit and Telegram doing scams, but I had no association with those fake accounts so I wasn't worried about that. They were more interested in McAfee, the SEC stuff and the endorsement stuff. I had already tweeted out everything that happened with me and John and I talked about it on YouTube so there wasn't anything new I could tell them that was different to what was already out there. No, that was not an exciting door knock.

I didn't want to get involved. They subpoenaed me and had a warrant for the phone that I had when I visited McAfee. The phone was bricked when the FBI got it, so they couldn't get any data off of it and the cell phone services only store text messages for a certain number of months. Only the other week, I guess since now John is dead, they closed the case. My lawyer called me and said, "They're going to return your phone." Now to call my lawyer is $500 an hour. He called to say that my broken iPhone 7 is going to be returned to me, but my broken iPhone is not even worth as much as the lawyer charged.

WHACKD – John created the cryptocurrency $WHACKD, had a tattoo that said $WHACKD and posted a tweet saying that he would not commit suicide. Do you think John was WHACKD?

XVG Whale – My initial reaction when I heard the news was, I thought he committed suicide. Maybe he was so used to the life of partying that prison would not be fun for him as he was getting older. So, my initial reaction was that he killed himself. But then, I was looking at some stuff on your timeline, the interview with Janice about how they haven't released the autopsy, the death certificate and that sort of thing. I think there's a possibility that he was WHACKD, so my opinion has changed.

WHACKD – What was your reaction when you heard the news of John's death?

XVG Whale – As self-centred as it sounds, I was sort of relieved because I didn't want to be subpoenaed to testify in a US trial against

John when he was extradited. I didn't want to be seen as a snitch type of figure because if I'm subpoenaed to testify then legally, I have to. So, you know in a selfish self-centred way, it was a sigh of relief as I knew John was involved with all types of different things. I had mixed feelings about it all.

WHACKD – We spoke previously and you mentioned John's cars, can you elaborate a little on that?

XVG Whale – Yeah, so I sent you the pictures of that car in McAfee's garage, that old school Mustang or charger or whatever it was. He had that because it didn't have logical components and McAfee strongly believed that at some point in time, there was going to be an EMP set off by nukes to shut off the energy grid. McAfee strongly believed in that apocalyptic scenario, and he told me that's why he had that car, so if the electricity stopped working, then his car would still work. He also had a bunch of guns and he was like, "We're set, we got all these guns and stuff everyone else is just going to be our slaves."

WHACKD – Yeah, it's a very nice car. Did John share any other notable stories with you?

XVG Whale – Yeah, John told a story about how he would play Russian roulette with a revolver. I think that's how he got respect from some people in South America. He would do that with a bullet in the gun, point it to his head, and pull the trigger. I think it was a bit of a thing he did, he never did it in front of me but my theory is if he did that, maybe he had a bullet with no powder in it, or maybe he used the wrong calibre so the pin wouldn't actually fire, or he was just crazy and he would actually do that.

WHACKD – How would you summarise your overall experience with John?

XVG Whale – McAfee was one crazy motherfucker. I didn't really think about it going over to visit him and it was cool, but I partially regret it because of all that drama. It stressed my girlfriend out, she was like "What have you got us involved with?" especially after the FBI came and stuff like that. I was super happy and doing well before I met McAfee. I still would have been doing my thing in the crypto space without that connection. Yes, it helped my clout some, but at the same time, it wasn't exactly worth it in regard to the drama. It affected my personal relationships and then there's the court stuff. I didn't know a whole lot about it beforehand, I just went there, so I have a lot of mixed feelings about the guy. Whatever happened, I do hope Janice can get closure.

Chapter Seven
Paul Flanagan

WHACKD – Thanks for doing this, can you introduce yourself and briefly describe when you first became aware of John McAfee?

Paul Flanagan – Sure. I'm Paul Flanagan and I was the sole developer for John McAfee's Bitcoin Play in 2019. I had been aware of John for a long time, but mostly due to using his anti-virus software. But, before knowing I was going out to meet him, I didn't really know a great deal about him.

WHACKD – How did the idea start to create a game with John come around?

Paul Flanagan – By the time I was in contact with McAfee I had already built a few mobile applications which helped to serve as our proof-of-concept, one of which was an idea to crowdsource charity payments using the application's ad revenue. Essentially, the idea was that a user could pick a charity and then see the contributions they were making as they played the game. So, I met a guy called Jamie Edwards, he was very entrepreneurial and also looking to get into crypto at that time. We took some of the programmes that I was making and modified them to be more crypto-based and then we contacted McAfee over Twitter, and we sent him some ideas of ours along with the proof-of-concept piece that we created and then John invited us out to meet with him in the Bahamas, which was when I first met him. Before meeting John, I was very much the silent partner and the communications were handled by Jamie. If you spent 20 minutes researching John McAfee you could easily conclude that you may not want him to have your telephone number. But we had an idea of what we wanted to present to John and so we adapted the charity elements and turned it into a quiz game. At the time we were beta testing the app around a bunch of my friends and others here in the UK, I had to pay a guy £20 to do the UI, which is funny looking back.

WHACKD – So when you left England for the Bahamas what was that like?

Paul Flanagan – Well, when we were invited over to meet with John, my wife was sure we were getting catfished. Nonetheless, Jamie and I booked the flights and we were out in full adventure mode. We initially flew to Philadelphia and had a layover of about eight hours. I remember it being about midnight and I had slept on a bench at the Airport before jumping on a flight to Miami, then we finally travelled on another flight to Exuma. When we arrived at the airport it was tiny, I still don't know how a full-sized aeroplane could land there, but it did.

We then got a taxi into Georgetown, I was in charge of the plane tickets and Jamie was in charge of where we were staying, but for whatever reason when we got there, we didn't have anywhere to stay. We just wandered around Georgetown each with a massive suitcase trying to find a hotel and then we found Choppies Bar, the hotels were like $200 a night, and we didn't have that kind of cash on us. In total, we only had like $500 between us and on Exuma, it doesn't go very far.

We rocked up to the bar and John wasn't there, he was off the island at the time when we arrived. We spoke to Choppy and then he disappeared after he heard that we had nowhere to stay. We were working out whether or not we could pitch a tent on the beach or something and then Choppy came back and said "It's all taken care of, I'll put you in John's room." It was two minutes around the corner and it was a nice little chalet on the marina, I think the jetlag caught up with us because I had one beer and then crashed out to sleep

The next day I booted up my computer to check that everything was working and we soon realised that Exuma didn't have any sort of ad coverage for the Unity ads. I tried to fix the issue and then the app stopped running, I started to make some changes and then my computer just went bang, and it was dead. I've still got no idea what the hell killed it, but the computer was dead.

I had no sort of backup on me for the unity stuff either but luckily, we did have a version of the app running on our phones so that was the only way we could show it, we couldn't demonstrate any of the code or anything in the background, so that was kind of the state of things. I also remember Choppy decided to feed a bunch of sharks, he would bang his blade on this chock to cut up chicken and then throw it in the water and the sharks would all come up to eat, I am petrified of the sea, and sharks.

WHACKD – What was your first interaction with John like?

Paul Flanagan – So, about two hours after the computer had killed itself, we were sat on the top balcony of the bar and I remember Jamie shouting "Oh, dude, he's here!" I sit up and look over the side and there's John, he looked like the guy from the beginning of Jurassic Park, like this white suit, the white hat, and he's got a cane. That's what John looked like. We waved down to him and he waved back, when he was close enough, he said "When you guys are ready, join me on the boat" and he gestured out towards the boat so we dump the laptop in our room, grab our phones, and walk out to where he was docked.

The dock itself seemed to get smaller and smaller as it went out towards where the boat was. Now, bear in mind we had just watched a bunch of sharks feeding in those waters. So, it was not only nerve-racking because we were walking up to go meet the guy, but it was more because I was also trying my best not to fall into the water and die. When we got to the boat, we were invited in and John was doing something at the time so we sat and had a beer whilst stroking the dogs, just waiting for John to be finished with whatever he was doing.

The whole pitch to John was to advertise the app and to ask him to provide narration for it, we asked him to record some vocals samples which we could chop up and use within the app. There was a Bahamian guy with a shotgun, Big Steve, there was another guy with a machine gun and John also had his handgun in his lap. Since then, when I'm pitching to a client, I might say, I've been through a pitch surrounded by guys with guns next to John McAfee, not much can faze me after that.

WHACKD – Did John have any larger plans for the application? Or was it just an amusement?

Paul Flanagan – So, yeah, he did have bigger things that he wanted to do with the app. There were certain features that he was describing, although, the more we went into the evening the more alcohol we all consumed. I remember one idea John wanted to implement was to have access to a list of everyone that was connected to the app so he could then click on one of the users and just begin to talk to them. He wanted to inject that into someone's experience, to have a one-on-one conversation with them. I had to suggest we leave that idea for a future version though as we were so far away from that point.

There were so many features and plans he wanted to integrate though, there was the idea of getting John into the metaverse and bringing AI into some of those sorts of pieces as well. At that point in time, it was something said more in jest but we released the first version and it was one of the top three quiz games on the Google Playstore, it hit the top three trending in the first week and a half, which was really cool.

WHACKD – What was the launch of the project like and what events led to the project being shut down after its initial success?

Paul Flanagan – What shut it down was John getting arrested in a South American country. In the lead-up to that though, after the initial meeting took place me and Jamie left the Bahamas and came back to the UK. Jamie then flew back out there to spend some more time with John and by that point I was working from home, making all the updates, adding John's vocals and making sure everything else John had wanted was sorted before launch and everything was going okay, to an extent. I was the sole developer working full time trying to fix the bugs in live time, during that whole launch period.

I remember it was the very next day after Jamie came back to the UK from the Bahamas, where John sailed into the Dominican Republic and was then detained. I remember someone quoted that: "he had enough munitions on the boat to invade the entire country." He was detained there for a while and because he had dual citizenship with the USA and the UK, he was able to get deported to London, it was at that point of him getting arrested that basically he said to projects that he was involved with, you know, shut everything down.

WHACKD – Can you share any memorable moments from your time in the Bahamas with John?

Paul Flanagan – Yeah, well while I was out with John, I had the attitude that nothing could hurt me. On one of the days out there was a knock on the door, someone said "John wants to see you on the boat" and so we wandered down. John's there and he's got this dinghy, it's this little white thing with an engine and John's like "We're going for a trip" and I'm like "Okay, I'm not good with water, or sharks, even on the best of days." Nonetheless, five of us clambered onto this thing and he sailed us all out to a local island.

There's footage in the Netflix documentary that recently came out with some of the mobile phone footage that I shot while on that boat. Anyway, so John sails out to this island and the only thing on there is a bar, we sat and drank there for some hours. I do have some audio recordings from that time but we must have drunk about $600 worth of alcohol before all getting back on the boat. I don't know what the drink-driving laws are for boats, but we sailed right out into the ocean and then he just cuts the engine, and we just sat there.

I couldn't help wondering 'Am I going to end up in the sea right now' but I think he was just enjoying the view, I'm not a fan of the water, and in this dinghy, I was just holding on for dear life but after that, we circled back and went back to Johns Yacht, that was a cool day overall, apart from the whole fearing for my life while we were out there.

WHACKD – During that time, John was also gearing up for his 2020 US presidential campaign did you see anything regarding that during your stay?

Paul Flanagan – Yeah, so on the first day we were there he did this big interview with some American network, they were in New York, in Times Square, and we were all just sat there watching him do it. He was being interviewed via his phone, and he also had these little masks that people were wearing, and they all had John McAfee's Face on them, can see us there at that time on his Twitter, it was a surreal experience.

WHACKD – After being arrested in the Dominican Republic, John was later departed to London before going travelling around Europe. Did you have any further communication with John during any of that period? Do you have any notable stories from when you met him?

Paul Flanagan – After he was deported from what I remember he just went completely off the grid; I had no idea where he was at that time. I do remember his stories though; he was a great storyteller. He spoke about how an ex-girlfriend tried to shoot him in the head but failed, she put the gun to his head whilst he was sleeping and because her hand was shaking as she turned her head and pulled the trigger she missed and that blew out his eardrum. He also spoke about these SAS-type scuba men that invaded his place in Belize and some other wild stuff, there was just story after story, and it was all very interesting.

WHACKD – John claimed on Twitter around that time that he had 31 terabytes of incriminating data on members of the government, do you have any thoughts or comments on that?

Paul Flanagan – Oh, I wouldn't be surprised if that was all linked, one of the things that I expected after his death was a massive leak. I expected it to be on like a Deadman switch, where it would trigger upon his death and everything that he had would be made public. I mean there was some odd crypto activity when he died, but nothing substantial came out in the end.

WHACKD – In June of 2021, it was reported that John committed suicide in jail, what did you think of this when you heard this news?

Paul Flanagan – Well, it was a real shock and I was very saddened to hear it. It was during all the COVID stuff and I had essentially turned the news off for about six months at that point then one day a friend texted me to say that John had died and that he had committed suicide. Well, in some ways I think it could sort of makes sense, I mean he had been a like playboy for 50 years, and I think he knew he wouldn't be getting out of prison again, either way, it's a really sad situation.

WHACKD – The Spanish authorities are still holding his body; do you have any comments or thoughts on that?

Paul Flanagan – I think it's truly terrible. Janice deserves some sort of closure, you know. I haven't spoken with her in a long time but I do hope that the authorities stop fucking around and that she gets what she needs from them.

WHACKD – During the short time that you had known John, did he change your outlook or perspective in any particular way? And if so, can you share how?

Paul Flanagan – He was able to make me feel a lot more adventurous and outgoing in the world. I was very much naturally introverted and reserved to my computer and coding, but by actively going out and seeing the world and seeing how he lived in the Bahamas and then launching Bitcoin play with him, it all opened up my outlook and attitude to life.

He also gave me a little quiz, he wanted to gauge how intelligent I was, he asked how to solve this problem, it was like you've got two bytes, and you want to switch them, but you don't have any sort of buffer, how do you do this? It was a very old issue from when computers were basically just circuit boards with very little else going on with them, it's hard to hard to describe. It was this XOR switch solution which he had written down on a piece of paper and he signed it and then he had given it to me. I still have that paper out in my office, along with a signed McAfee mask as well, I'm grateful to him for all of that.

Chapter Eight
Rob Loggia

WHACKD – Hi Rob, thank you for doing this. Can you introduce yourself and briefly describe when you first became aware of John McAfee?

Rob Loggia – I'm Rob Loggia, I was the campaign manager for John's 2020 presidential campaign and a core team member for his 2016 campaign. The second part of your question is kind of a three-part answer.

I first heard of McAfee when I was a kid before computers were just picking up. McAfee's software must have just come out around then. I didn't have a PC, I had a Commodore 64, but a friend of mine had a PC. He had gotten the McAfee Antivirus and said something at the time about the guy that owned the company, but that just got filed away and I didn't use the product. Then obviously it became bigger from there.

Then fast forward to the Belize period. I was working at the time and I remember being in the car having lunch and the radio was on. They were talking about the news surrounding John, you know the police situation, the flight, and everything else. I just remember sitting there like "Oh wow, that's wild, that's the antivirus guy." By then everybody had heard of him and I was like "Man, I kinda hope he gets away, sounds like a wild story," and then he did.

Fast forward again years later to just before we met and John declared his intention to run for president, I remembered him from those years before. So, those are the three parts going back to when I was very young when I heard his name. It didn't mean much to me at the time, but there it was.

WHACKD – Before being in contact with John, were there any other memorable moments from his early life that come to mind?

Rob Loggia – There wasn't really, just this sense that he's on the run and he says he's innocent. I'm always going to sympathise with that position. When we look at the idea of law and then the actual implementation of it, it's one of the biggest problems. Everybody likes to say it's the cost of living in a society, but that's just to paper over that problem.

Once you set up law, you set up these edifices of power, you create instruments that innocent people are going to be beaten with. To not be sympathetic to that seems strange to me. Yet it seems the majority of people just dismiss the importance of the fact that the law can be used as a weapon of persecution. So, I just naturally sympathised with that. My first major exposure to him, though, was when he announced on Greta Van Susteren, I think that was the show, that he intended to run for president back in 2016.

WHACKD – What was your first direct communication with John?

Rob Loggia – Shortly after that, I had been separately running a campaign to try and draft, that is, to call into service, Charlie Sheen, to run for president. I had several months of that already and the season was getting a little riper but Charlie was nowhere to be found. Shortly after that, he announced that he had AIDS, so I guess he had other shit on his mind, understandably. So, my efforts to reach him had failed and I had accepted that. I didn't expect much to come of it and I certainly didn't expect to run Charlie Sheen and have him win.

It was more about making a statement about certain things that were important to me, one of them being to elect anyone other than a career politician: just somebody who didn't give a fuck, who would go in there and be honest if they were elected by the American people. I thought that was all you could ask for at this point; good leadership over something that's fundamentally broken is a misnomer. So, to look to elect leaders, we should not be looking for elected leaders. We need to first elect exposers of people, those that are going to show us what is being done in positions of power. Then, the reformers, for lack of a better word: people that will clean that up. Whether this happens is anybody's guess, but that was the idea.

I had been working on all this stuff separately already and I had to wonder if I could throw my support, along with the work that I had done in conjunction with that campaign, if it could be reapplied to another campaign, the artwork and some slogan ideas that I had for effective communicating and such, so I was just kind of on the lookout.

I do not watch the news, but I was at my brother's the one night it was on the TV and there was John, he was talking about the fact he intended to run for president. They made a video with a green screen and the message resonated with me one hundred percent, so at that point, I just showed up. That's where our contact began.

WHACKD – When you first met John, how were you received? Do you remember the initial interactions?

Rob Loggia – Oh, yes, I do. The first time we physically met I was picking him and Janice up from an airport and then taking them back to a hotel in New Jersey for some Libertarian Party campaign work. I was to meet them at the airport and then take them to the hotel that they were staying at for a convention the next day that we were all going to attend, where I was received as a cartel hitman.

At that point, we hadn't met, but I knew John certainly had a lot of strange dealings in the world, and the people he had associations with weren't all necessarily some of the best people, and some of them very trustworthy people, whatever. Some people that had his number certainly weren't in any of the above.

Then there's me, who up till then, you know, just very generous I guess you can call it. I just wanted to help. I didn't demand payment and I had already secured my campaigning funds through three years of work and saving. I had built the cushion from which to do that. So, it wasn't an immediate issue of being paid. It was just like "Let's get the thing done," and I think he appreciated that, but it does raise certain questions. It's not a common thing and I have what some people might call a darker appearance. I can't help that. I have dark hair, brown eyes, and a rather severe face with a strong cut to it and the way I dress is the way I dress. So, John took a look at the total package and wondered if I wasn't there to kill him, which was his first reaction. Because he was such an open-minded man, he didn't make his mind up about these things, he just kind of went with it when he had a feeling. He allowed things to continue to happen, he did that with me as I watched him do it with many other people after that. With us, it led to a friendship. In other cases, it led directly into the dark places he anticipated, so I guess it's a hit-or-miss thing once you get there.

WHACKD – Was there anything particularly notable about that first car ride with John?

Rob Loggia – Well, one funny story from when I picked them up in the car is I got lost on the way back to the hotel. I took a wrong turn onto a highway, we had to do this whole loop around, I could tell both Janice and John were very uncomfortable in the backseat and his security guy was nervous in the front seat and everybody was kind of just looking at me. It finally occurred to me that nobody was smoking. I knew John smoked as I'd seen he was often smoking on social media, so I'm just like "You know, you can smoke if you want. I wasn't smoking just to be polite." All these people smoke, why am I not smoking? So, we all just lit up and it was like this big sigh of relief and we all started chatting at that point, but the first 20 minutes, especially when driving around aimlessly, the tension, you could have cut it with a knife. Despite the reputation that some people have seemed to have saddled John with, he was not impulsive about his reactions, he just watched to see what would happen.

WHACKD – In 2016 John sought to form the Cyber Party, what happened with that?

Rob Loggia – Yeah, that was his first go. There were some problems with the leadership team there, and the campaign manager was ultimately sent to jail for outright fraud. Unfortunately, the party was a non-starter and even if the problems that existed hadn't been there, it would have still been a non-starter.

Ultimately, if John was serious about getting his message out, which he was, it was likely he was going to wind up on the doorstep of the Libertarian Party. They are the only relevant party that has 50 years of groundwork into building any type of platform, weak as it is.

WHACKD – In 2016, John publicly challenged the FBI on CNN, volunteered to decrypt the San Bernardino iPhone, and participated in the first-ever nationally televised Libertarian Party debate. Additionally, the hacker group Anonymous wanted him to become Donald Trump's security adviser. What are your thoughts on that period? Do you have a personal highlight from that time?

Rob Loggia – Yeah, life just sort of blows past. I mean, you wake up each day and you're like "What the fuck is this?" That's the best way I can describe that period. Suddenly you find yourself in the thick of it. I mean, you have to understand my background was nothing very interesting. I've had a long life and it's interesting to me, but I don't expect it would be to anybody else.

When I set out campaigning in 2015 it was after walking out of a job. I was a middle manager at a company whose name most people would recognise, which I will not share, but the point is: it was an entirely new world for me. It all happened very quickly, I was watching a lot of these things happen and not knowing what they meant, not knowing the significance of it all.

So, you see something like the stuff with the iPhone, for example, or directly challenging the FBI live on TV like that. Somebody like me, who had lived an ordinary life, might look at that and say it is was just grandstanding and not see it for the inherently dangerous activity that it was. It took some adjusting to that in the realisation that, wow, this guy's not just up there talking, he's subjecting himself to very real dangers, because of the extreme nature of his message. Getting it out there, it was the equivalent of painting a target on your back.

Talk about how naive I was when we first began to collaborate on his first campaign. One of the first things I said to him on the phone was "Okay, I will help you but you have to understand that it's my opinion that if somebody like you were to be elected, something not very good would probably happen there shortly afterwards. And, you know, all efforts would be made to either neutralise or eliminate you, I cannot prove that, but it's what I think." I had already seen enough of him by then to know he was not someone that would be easily neutralised at all, so that leaves one alternative for those that wanted to shut him up: they would have to do something to him. So, I was like "Are you comfortable with that? Because I can't have that on my conscience. You have to understand that." I was just giving him an out, saying like "If you didn't think about how far this could go, maybe now you should." At the time, he almost laughed at me and had every right to; he was already up to his neck deep in that shit.

He expressed to me in very kind terms that he did not mind taking those risks but it became very real to me. What I started to see as a possibility, he already knew was a very distinct reality. That was the most jarring thing, around that time it was very exciting, but the stuff we were doing was very fucking intense and it took a toll on me, medically. I had issues with my health and you know, it's not like it all comes for free, I guess is what I'm trying to say.

WHACKD – Through the 2016 to 2019 period, is there anything, in particular, you wish to go over from those years?

Rob Loggia – Well, my best memories are from those years. A couple of times we got to spend time not related to anything that was being done externally. There were a lot of disappointments too. I know there are people out there who are always going to believe that John was trying to run some kind of scam with the company MGT that he became the CEO of. I'm not going to deny that others had that on their minds because there were, and I met many of them. But John wasn't one of them, he was extremely passionate about the company. It was a big heartbreak to him, and me, with what happened there. The products that we had all spent time working on never got to see the light of day, because of the shenanigans of other people and the manoeuvrings of government agencies. A combination of the two proved fatal, so that dream was never realised, but it wasn't for want of trying.

Aside from that, though, the strongest way that I remember John was as a personal friend, it'll always be that way. I have very few close friends, and so did he. Probably none, some people who are close to him would say. So that was unique for both of us to be able to do that. Thankfully I'm blessed with a world full of people that I care about, and love. But in some ways, there's always a distance, and it has to do with the way that we look at the world. John was just one of the few people I've met that looked at a lot of things the same way as I do and arrived at similar conclusions about people, about the way they function, what they're up to, you know, what we're doing here. Even just admitting that we don't have the answers to that was a big thing that he and I shared. We talked about stuff like that for hours at times. The basis for the friendship was intellectual, it was not anything else. That's what I remember the most: how we were able to cement our friendship during the sleepier times in that period.

WHACKD – During John's 2020 US presidential run you were his campaign manager whilst he was in exile in the Bahamas and Cuba. What unique situations did you find yourself in as a result of that?

Rob Loggia – Oh, those were crazy times. Probably the most unique situation that I never could have anticipated was being on the phone with the British Embassy in the Dominican Republic. They had locked them up there. The United States Embassy didn't want anything to do with it. They wouldn't even send anybody, which is interesting because it's not like they were looking to pick him up at that time, so that was strange. I was talking to the lady without much information at all. It's not like I was kept in the loop on everything and John ran his show. People don't seem to grasp that, even when he had roomfuls of assistants, he still ran his own show. I only ever knew what I needed to know, and I was fine with that. I don't see why anybody should ever not be fine with that. But this was not something that I was prepared for, which is to say she's asking me questions and I just don't have the answers. I'm like "Listen, you've just got to get down there, he's a British citizen being held without cause and they're not respecting their own laws at this point!"

She then actually got pretty hot with people and from what I understand they had somebody down there within the hour, so it was the British Embassy that got him out from the Dominican Republic confinement and I played the role of intermediary for that. You asked for the most standout thing, that was one of the oddest fucking things I've ever had to do.

WHACKD – How did John's 2020 political campaign differ from his 2016 run?

Rob Loggia – Well, first of all, he was telling people not to vote for him, that was the whole thrust of the campaign: "Don't Vote McAfee." It was our final expression of the absurdity of it all, which was plenty present in the 2016 campaign, but more subtle because there was other work we were trying to do. It was a holler to the futility of people jumping from one side to the other, elections being decided by this very slippery middle, that is so superficial and tied to almost nothing that it just makes the process as simple as "We own both sides" and that's it, we're done. But it was a fun campaign and we weren't under pressure to try to prove ourselves to anyone. I think you saw we were able to express ourselves more freely.

Out of the two campaigns, because it was two campaigns that John ran in 2016, I preferred his platform and tone and tenor in the Cyber Party campaign. Coming to know him I feel that expressed more of his viewpoint whereas he tended to focus on things that were more important to that Libertarian Party audience. Not to say that he misrepresented himself, these were very real elements of his personality, but there was a lot more to him than just those libertarian talking points.

I think those other things came out more clearly in the 2016 campaign, and I like to believe that they also came out more clearly in the 2020 campaign. So as far as messaging, I think we did a lot better there and I guess that what would stand out the most in my mind, was that overall impression of John. There are a lot of videos that he posted on Twitter from that time. I mean, he made a body of work that showed so much of what he had been trying to get across all these years with his extreme behaviour, which he would never deny was extreme. He understood people behaving like him did not scale, that if everybody behaved like John McAfee, we couldn't have a society, he understood that.

He wasn't trying to create a world full of John McAfee's. He was trying to make a point to a world full of ordinary people: maybe if they just did some things a little differently there would be a lot fewer problems for everybody, and the world would be more resilient to the few Johns McAfee's that it had to suffer because I tell you there won't be many.

WHACKD – John was detained in the Dominican Republic and later deported to London. Do you have any thoughts or stories to share from that time?

Rob Loggia – You know, that time was a difficult one for everybody involved. They were living in some hellish conditions. A very nice boat with too many people on it and out on the ocean like that really isn't pleasant. I probably knew about as much as the public at any given time. On that one occasion where I was contacted with the favour to handle the embassy, it wasn't because I knew what was going on from minute to minute — I didn't. I had to trust and have faith that they would see their way through, as I had no visibility as to their movements or what they were doing or where they intended to go. When they would tweet that they were in port someplace it was news to me along with everybody else.

WHACKD – In June of 2021, it was reported that John committed suicide in jail. What was initial your reaction to this?

Rob Loggia – My reaction? That's hard to quantify. Scepticism, I guess. The first account I saw of it was more or less all there was: not enough at all for me to form any kind of opinion, let alone a strong opinion or have an emotional reaction. So, at that point, it was more or less just scepticism and a desire to find out what was happening.

WHACKD – What are your thoughts on the alleged suicide?

Rob Loggia – Well, okay, since then, time has passed and you find out other things. It's just a matter of looking at what is public. There's no need for anybody to tell any secrets, not that I have any, and just based on the public information, and maybe one piece of information that isn't public, it became impossible for me to accept that story.

I didn't immediately rule it out either. I'm not going to tell you some bullshit, like, oh, you know, he loved the life and that there's some reason why he would never be capable of that. We're all capable of that, and the worst of things. I mean, everything Genghis Khan did, I could have done, you could have done, if the circumstances were different. If our upbringing was different, and maybe slightly different chemicals in our heads and we were dropped in a completely different time period. You or I might have done that. We're all human, so I wasn't prepared to say that it couldn't be.

If he had thought there was no way out, I believe he was capable of it. And I believe that I might have done the same in that situation, and that would be to deny the hangman his pleasure. I could see that. I could even respect that, and I wouldn't hold that against him for doing that, even though I do miss him. If he felt like there was undue humiliation or, any other sense of worse coming, and he had exhausted all avenues — and this is an important thing about John if he had exhausted all avenues of basically avoiding that fate — sure. I believe he was capable of it, of course, he was, and I think anybody honest with themselves would see that they could have done that too.

However, I just don't think that's the case. You have to understand, this is all public information, anybody can go look this up. John had a barrel full of appeals remaining so it would have been years before he would ever hit the shores of the United States. Now, I can understand wanting to avoid that at all costs, however, the costs were several years in the distance. John was 76, a lifelong smoker. I think he would have hedged the bet and just fought them. Not wanting to live out that time in jail, okay, but he could have fought that too, and I think he would have.

It doesn't make sense when you add the fact that people were gunning for him from numerous walks of life. Frankly, though, it seems like he was perhaps gotten there — if he's dead, which I believe he is. I've heard enough to accept that and to take it more or less as fact at this point.

WHACKD – In June 2019, John claimed on Twitter that he had 31 terabytes of incriminating information on world governments. Do you have any thoughts on this?

Rob Loggia – It was funny, there were people who jumped on my Twitter shortly after John's death, and they were all tweeting at my account, like "Where's that data?" Like, I don't fucking know. John had lots of things but I only knew what I needed to know, and that wasn't something that concerned me. One time he had asked me to tweet about it over his account and identify that it was me. He gave me his Twitter credentials, and I posted, and then he changed his credentials back after, but it wasn't something that I had any direct knowledge of. That isn't to say that it existed or that it didn't exist. There were many different times that many things were made apparent to me that I was completely unaware existed beforehand.

There's a type of thinking common in the spy world, if you want to call it that, the Secret Service, military and everything else: the idea of compartmentalization. If John was looking at that problem, he would say "How much of this can I do myself? Do I need somebody to function the Dead Man's Switch? Does anybody else other than that person need to know who that is? No. Does anybody else even need to know that I have it?" That's the way he would proceed. I suspect that if there was a Dead Man's Switch, and if a person was operating it, that's the way he would have looked at it.

I will also add that things were said to me that led me to believe he had quite a bit of data, I'll just put it that way. Very specific things. I do believe that things existed at some point, and whether or not they were stored someplace I think the only person that knows is the person he would have asked to look after them. Now I'll say for the record it wasn't me. That person could be dead, and that person could be any number of things. They could be incarcerated. They could have lost that data and any number of things could have happened. Nothing's perfect so not having it surface doesn't mean that he didn't have that plan or intention.

There was also talk about a building that collapsed in Florida and it was speculated the data might have been there. Some people say that, but I have no way to confirm or deny that. I have no information that people may think I have.

Our basis was one of friendship. We were involved with the campaigns, but we became friends first. If you were sitting down for a few beers with somebody, you wouldn't want to talk about a lot of other shit that you had to do the rest of the time, so it was kind of like that: we talked about other stuff.

WHACKD – Are you able to speak about Janice's current situation? Do you have any comments on the Spanish authorities still withholding John's body?

Rob Loggia – She is continuing to fight for information. She has been very transparent about everything that she can be. She is more protective of her actual movements and location and we all need to respect that. I don't ask her where she is at any given time and nobody should if they care about her.

But it's been over a year and the police reports and basic information have not been released. To say that's odd would be an understatement. Frankly, in that amount of time, they could change anything they wanted within that report. People may say "Oh, who would falsify a report?" but a report is what they make of it. It's what they give you minus any redactions that they care to make. They can be public redactions, or they can be private redactions. You can redact something with a black magic marker, but when you're the government, you can redact it so it was never on the paper. They've now had that length of time that anything they produced would probably pass any scrutiny; they're in charge of making the originals.

It's so sus at this point that I don't see how anybody can accept anything they say. And yet, most people, the important ones, all will accept it, and life goes on. I feel bad when I talk about this, because I'm not saying to give up, and I'm not saying I don't have a lot of respect for what Janice is doing, I'm merely stating I believe the ship has sailed on actually discovering something or capturing it. There's a reason why when you're operating a sting you don't want them to know beforehand: you don't want to give them time to prepare, the more time they have to put things together the more plausible what they come back with will be. Whereas if you catch them while things are still happening, maybe the papers you collect there have something written down that wasn't supposed to be and you can capture that, that's when the world gets a leak. But, if they have time, just like any criminal organisation they can paper over it, and the way they do it is going to be more convincing than anybody can disprove as a private citizen because they control the printing press to make this shit.

I don't know anything that can be said at this point other than that he's most likely deceased and he most likely didn't kill himself. Those are the two things that I sit here believing.

WHACKD – During the time that you knew John, did he change your outlook or perspective in any way? If so, how?

Rob Loggia – I mean, more than I could mention. We were passionate about many of the same ideas. One thing I learned from John, and I say learned because it was for me, is this: before I met John, 'ideas' could be enough to lead to separation from people. One of the things I learned from John is that sometimes that's avoidable, but we have to make some kind of effort to fight against it, to talk across the aisle. Maybe we can't do it for our bitterest of personal enemies as that's a tough pill to swallow, but for ideological enemies, for people that just disagree with us and for people who don't seek to harm us but just see the world radically different from us, we have to try to look across and see the person sitting there, otherwise, everything else is for nought.

There's no point in pursuing to improve the world if we're going to turn our backs on all the people that we're supposedly trying to improve it for. So many people, including myself in the past, fall into that trap. Pink Floyd called it 'the turning away,' when you just turn your back and you don't want to see anymore. It's tempting because the world is a lot less hurtful if you do it.

John taught me one of the places that it comes from, one of the wellsprings, the vortex to the dimension of evil if you will. The foothold by how it gets in is to look at somebody else and see them as no longer human, so all these things that would ordinarily be terrible, have suddenly become okay for me to do to them. John taught me to see that and to stop doing it myself. I will always appreciate him for that because I do feel that it has made me a better person.

WHACKD – Do you have any other comments or stories you'd like to share?

Rob Loggia – I would like to say that one of the things we did share is the two of us spent most of our lives being completely misunderstood by most of the people around us. It's one of the things we shared and it's one of the things we joked about. You know, he was the king of illusion, he used a lot of illusion and gained benefit from it.

There were many times when people would paint him as a monster and I would know a story, some simple story, but something that displayed the fundamental humanity of the man, I would want to tell it — but then I would have to stop because I wanted to respect his need to operate in very difficult circles that I couldn't begin to understand, and I didn't want to get in the way of that.

But, the sensitive part of me wanted to speak up and say, you know, this man whom you're trashing, well this is what I've seen, and I'm full of those stories but I'm not going to tell them all.

WHACKD – Would you mind sharing one of those stories with me here in the series?

Rob Loggia – One I will share: we were all on one the few vacations that we all got to take and this time I was able to bring my wife, along with John, Janice and my daughter were with us, and all of John's entourage. We had spent the whole day going around doing different things that had been planned. We went to the pirates' cove, shopping, and other different things. It was a whole day full of adult shit.

So, John stops everything towards the middle of the afternoon. He gets his whole entourage in the car and we all drive to the movie theatre. We find a kid's flick. This is all for my daughter. I think he passed out halfway through and got some rest which he needed, but John, Janice, and the entire security team all sat there and watched 'The Incredibles.' It was the closest thing in the theatre to something someone my daughter's age would like and that we could also watch without shooting ourselves.

What I want to highlight here, is that my daughter's always a good sport, she wasn't complaining, and she was enjoying herself along with the adults, but they were still adult things, and John was sensitive enough to pick up on that. Without being asked, without being told, without being complained to, for him to consider somebody else's plight, in this case, a child and say "Man if I was that child, I would want to do some kid thing now," and then to make it happen, that's the John I remember.

For people that are still capable of some measure of critical thought, all they need to do is watch the latest Netflix documentary. It's all right in there. Watch the surrounding cast of characters as they show the story, and you'll see constant expressing of concern with people's plight. John was asking "Are you okay?" or "Are you comfortable?"

and "This is what we're going to experience, are you all right with that?" He is constantly visibly concerned on the camera about everybody but himself, the entire time that this shit is mainly happening to him. For people not to understand that, after watching it, it's more of a statement on them and their inability to understand what they're being shown than it is on John. So, when they offer an opinion on John, other than getting mad or calling them names, I just have to tune it out. I mean, there's just no other alternative. I'll still see them as human beings but they haven't thought things through. I'd say 90% of the people that don't like him start their arguments in ways that make it clear they just haven't thought this stuff through.

WHACKD – That's my list of questions about done. Do you have anything else you would like to share?

Rob Loggia – I think the more important thing to John was the human side of the message. A word he often used in the first campaign was commonalities, finding them so that we can stand down the guns and maybe start to fix some shit and become better people. That was a very important part of the first campaign in 2016, it was ultimately who he was. He did not see himself as an angel or as someone who held himself up as an example for others to follow, behaviour-wise or otherwise. People that take it for that are making a big mistake in terms of understanding him. I say that for fans and foes alike. That was never his intent.

But the man invited danger and at that age, he was just a student of the human condition. He would keep somebody around that he knew was up to no good, just to see how low they would go with it, he wanted to know. Fucked up, I don't think I could live like that. When I identify a toxic person, I will take any steps necessary to eliminate them from my circle completely.

John used to be more like that when he was younger. He was very selective with whom he brought in at the company, and then he fled the United States and Colorado, after being surrounded by an entire colony of grifters. I think he became bored; he had lived a life of pure excitement and, like many who are fortunate enough to live to an older age, became very interested in the human condition.

I think that's one of the reasons he allowed it and wanted to watch it up close, to see what they would do. You know, what people do, if you understand that, I guess you can communicate better with others, and avoid some of the worst pitfalls. One of the ones he identified as a real problem was greed. When greed gets its hands on shit, man, it destroys everything, and this is from somebody who loves making money and promoted the idea of people making money. He evangelised the making of money but he hated greed, and I don't think a lot of people get that.

Chapter Nine
Mark Eglinton

WHACKD – Thanks for doing this, can you introduce yourself and describe when you first became aware of John McAfee?

Mark Eglinton – I'm Mark Eglinton, author and ghostwriter for different projects on many genres, music, sports, politics, and all that stuff. I knew about McAfee in the 1990s and vaguely followed him through the 2000s. I didn't think too much about what he was doing until he ended up in Belize and the news became a little bit disturbing. Then I followed it pretty closely until I engaged with John directly.

WHACKD – Before being in contact with John, what were your thoughts on his early life?

Mark Eglinton – Looking back, I always thought John was reasonably sane back when he was involved in tech. I think most people probably felt the same. It was only much later, from 2010 onwards, that it became obvious that there was much more to John than people knew before.

It was interesting because he was a guy who was really living by his own methods. However, I hate to say this, but it did feel like he was on a downward spiral from that point onward, and that turned out to be right.

WHACKD – After your first communication with John, what did you take away from the initial interactions?

Mark Eglinton – I didn't like him. The first communication we had was on Twitter by direct message and that moved pretty quickly to email. In the initial email dialogue, he wasn't very pleasant. He was suspicious, I get that. He'd been approached before by so many people and he'd worked with a couple of other guys on books before and so I think he was very guarded about getting involved with anyone else.

So, at first, I thought I didn't like him. I wasn't sure if I even wanted to do it because it was going to be difficult; I've had to work with difficult people before and sometimes it's just not worth it

But, things developed, when we first spoke on a video call he called me completely out of the blue, I was driving and pulled over into a petrol station, it was pouring rain on this Tuesday in winter and John was on the other end of the Skype video call.

From that point on, we had a pretty good relationship. It changed from there. I think he needed to see me and vice versa, I needed to see he was real. From that point onwards, it was pretty clear he was real.

WHACKD – As you began to get to know John, are there any little-known elements of his early life that were particularly impressive or shocking to learn?

Mark Eglinton – Well, it's funny, we didn't talk about his life in order, we decided pretty quickly on a few things: I was going to ghost-write his book, it was going to be his autobiography and he didn't want to be too involved with it in terms of how it was all put together.

He was happy to talk to me, and he talked to me about whatever he felt like talking about at any given time, it was up to me to piece it all together and extract the stuff that was important to steer the conversation. There wasn't any sort of structure to these conversations, it wasn't as though I said, "Okay, let's go back to your childhood and talk about that." He would just talk. I wasn't going to be able to dictate it. So, I just let him, but it was always completely random. We talked about the more recent stuff at first, he was on the run when we first got in contact so we talked about that.

It was after a few weeks that we got to his childhood and his early life. I didn't realise he had such a difficult childhood. He talked a lot about his father and how much he hated him. He was very keen to impress upon me that his upbringing had pretty well informed the rest of his life and I think that point was made in my book, once his father died, he decided to live life by his own rules, and that's how it went.

WHACKD – Did John speak much about his mother and father; can you speak a little more about that element of his early life?

Mark Eglinton – Very little, I remember him shutting me down quite seriously when I asked him about his mother, I asked "Once your dad died, did your mother meet anybody else?" I was just curious whether she remarried or had met someone else and he shut that down. He said, "I really don't want to discuss my mother's relationships." I was surprised by that.

John only ever mentioned his father in one conversation with me, it was a conversation about how abusive he was, and how he felt when he died. That was all we ever spoke about it.

WHACKD – After John made his millions and walked away from McAfee antivirus, what notable stories did he share from that period?

Mark Eglinton – The antivirus stuff is a bit of a myth because there are lots of numbers reported about how much John had made, I think the number is probably somewhere between 80 and 100 million, which is a lot, but people say he was a billionaire but he was nothing like that. He also didn't sell his company; he just got the benefit from the shares that he owned.

So, from that point onwards, he didn't want any part of the corporate life and this began the period where he got out of McAfee Antivirus, I saw an odyssey that encompassed several things; He got massively into jet-skiing, he would tell me great stories of him on the water, one of which is in my book, where he went across some bay and ran into a guy that had travelled from South America.

Shortly after that, he got into a yoga retreat, I challenged him on it and said "Listen, it sounds like you're just trying to pick up women" and initially he denied that, he said that wasn't the case but eventually he said, "Yeah, you're right" So, that's what it was, he was just hiding out in Colorado with this big house, bored and saw he could get athletic women to go and study there. I don't want to say it became a sort of cult, but it became a compound where John did pretty much what he wanted.

Then from there, he had an Aero-Trekking business that he got into, and that was the next thing. It was a pivotal time in his life because his nephew had crashed and died during a flight. John again denies that he left the US because of his nephew's death, there was also a lawsuit. I think that was probably what forced him to go. John would say differently, but I believe he left because of the pressure. From there he went to Belize and from there, it was all downhill.

WHACKD – What did you make of John's Belize saga, the laboratory, the story of officials extorting him, and the murder accusation involving Gregory Faull?

Mark Eglinton – I believe all that, but I don't think he killed Gregory Faull, I never did. I asked him directly. I asked him if he was involved in Gregory Faull's death and he told me he wasn't. Now, it was all very complicated down there and I'm not convinced I got the whole story, but I got a good portion of it.

There were lots of people double-crossing John. Some of his staff, some people that he knew in the government, there was a web of stuff going on down there. Several people were wanting to frame John and I believe somebody tried to frame John for Gregory Faull's murder.

Now, I don't approve of what happened to Gregory Faull in any way. But, do I think John was directly involved, on the balance of our conversations and from what I've read and heard, I would say no. I'm probably in the minority with that. More people believe that he did it than those who think he didn't.

WHACKD – What did you make of the alleged keystroke logging software on donated computers?

Mark Eglinton – Yeah, absolutely, true, I think he did that. I believe that was him getting back at the Belizean government in the way that he could, John knew how to do these things. So, I think that happened. I also think that explains why he was chased around the US once he got back.

He told me about being chased by cartels and all that stuff. I was never totally sure about that, about why was he chased by the Sinaloa Cartel. I think it's more likely somebody related to a Belizean government official was trying to get him back there.

Going back to the lab stuff, I think the lab stuff was all legitimate. This was something John was genuinely interested in, the anti-biotics, the anti-septic sprays and other stuff like that was something he really got into, I think that's proven by the fact that when he was raided by the GSU they didn't find any meth or anything else that they said they would find, I think John had a legitimate business.

WHACKD – During your talks with John, did he tell you any specific little-known stories about attempts on his life or times when he was in danger?

Mark Eglinton – Oh, yeah, I mean, I consider the period from when John Landed in Miami to when he left the US on a yacht as probably the most dangerous years of his life. Some of this was related to Janice because he met Janice the day he got back to the U.S. from Belize and at that time Janice was walking this tightrope between wanting to be with John and being loyal to her pimp.

I think about 50% of the time Janice was probably plotting against John. John had said that himself. She was trying to get John picked up, apprehended, whatever. She was with him the whole time and also had to go along with whatever was happening to him, which encompassed hiding in dumpsters in Portland while guys were looking for them John told me that he would lay in bed with one eye open and a finger on the trigger of a shotgun, whether that's bravado or not, I don't know. I do know that he had to stuff towels in the bullet holes in the wall of his house, which was in Tennessee.

People were trying to get in there, I think it was Janice's pimp. John had a loft in that house and Janice's pimp tried to get him. So, legitimately, I do think there were attempts on John's life at various times. Who they were by, I'm not sure. He said the Sinaloa Cartel pursued him by vehicle down through the Southwest too, whether it happened exactly like that I'm not sure, but yeah, there were people after him.

WHACKD – During your time ghost-writing for John's auto-biography he cancels the book deal, can you explain that event in greater detail and how it was resolved?

Mark Eglinton – Yeah, we had a deal with a publisher in the US, the same publisher who eventually published 'No Domain: The John McAfee Tapes' and things get to a point where a publisher needs to be able to contract directly with the subject. Wherever that's me, John, or whomever it is.

We had a significant deal and it was pretty well mapped out with all the deal points made. We got to the point where they were paying someone to create the contract and then sort the money for the advance and it took about a month to get that together. Sometime in the middle of all that John emailed me out of the blue. The email said 'Payment only in crypto.'

There were lots of expletives, 'there's no fucking way I'm dealing with money' and 'I haven't had a fucking bank in years' and all this stuff. I said, "Wait a minute, we never discussed this, you never at any point said that It would only be a crypto deal, this is a problem." And he said, "Well if it's a problem then fuck them, I'm not dealing with them."

I said, "This presents a problem for me now because I'm the one trying to get this deal together and you're telling me that you won't enter into it on the terms that we agreed?" He said, "Yeah that's how it is." So, there was that.

There was also the fact that there was no address to send John's contract to. I was like 'You have to be kidding' They were suggesting they needed a mailbox they could send it to, and they said, that it was what they needed, well that wasn't going to happen.

So, John just said "Forget it. Just leave it." So, I said to the publisher, without telling John at the time, I said, Listen, I'm thinking about doing this myself, repurposing what we have and trying to make it more of a biography or incorporate his voice. They were initially a little bit cautious about that. They feared legal issues, quite understandably. They insisted that I go back to John and get his permission, which, quite frankly, I didn't want to do.

I didn't know what he'd say, as it turned out, I emailed him and said 'Listen, I'm gonna try and write this book anyway, without you, it's gonna be a different format and you'll get no money. What do you think?' I expected him to write back and just abuse me, he said "Fine, Go ahead. I look forward to reading it when it comes out." I finally get back to the publisher and it's like John's gone, it's just me now. Let's get this done, so we did.

WHACKD – After talking with John in-depth; what do you think people misunderstand the most about him?

Mark Eglinton – I've gone through this so many times over the couple of years since he died and I think Johns a confusing mixture. On the one side, a good-hearted, kind guy, obviously, very intelligent. I do think he has a mean side, that's there. Whether that was caused by drugs when he was younger, I don't know.

He rerefers to a hallucinogenic episode that he had in the 70s as being this pivotal moment where the wiring in his brain was changed, I don't know enough about that stuff to know whether that can happen but something flips in him sometimes. I saw that a few times, it's like he had two personalities.

Certainly, the documentaries that have come out 'Running with the Devil' and the 'Gringo' both went into the dark side of John because it's better box office, and more exciting. I think the other side of John was more interesting, which is what I was trying to get to a lot of the time with the book I had written. I have audio recordings of John crying for like a minute at a time, just sobbing.

It's difficult to know what to say when you have this 74-year-old guy just crying on the phone to you, I don't think people knew that side of John. One reason is that he never showed it. I mean, if you set an interview up with John on YouTube or even on the news, John was showboating, always. He was grandstanding.

With me, I don't think he was doing that. He was being himself. I think that personality trait is one that people don't know, there was a very sensitive and caring person underneath the facade, but it was hard work getting there.

WHACKD – In 2019, John was on the run in the Bahamas, Cuba, and later in the Dominican Republic. Do you remember any memorable stories or conversations from that time?

Mark Eglinton – In the Dominican Republic, John claimed the CIA was there to pick them up. That might be true. He tells a story where he was on his Yacht and he pulled into a dock that was lined with Federal agents, or whoever they were, and they took their guns away from them. John told me that he made eye contact with this guy who was driving him to the police station or wherever they were going and from the moment John placed eyes on this guy he said he knew he was the CIA.

The CIA agent looked at John, as though he knew John knew he was CIA. He explained this kind of strange standoff, which made me think of the movie Heat, near the end of the film, where Robert De Niro and Al Pacino square off in a bar. De Niro's the criminal, Pacino's the cop that's been pursuing him forever and they sit there across the table and they have this conversation that reminded me of that, you know, here was the CIA trying to get McAfee, and McAfee trying not to be got, there was a mutual respect there.

In the end, John got out of the Dominican Republic, famously, somebody tried to bring him in and John ended up turning that back on some official in the Bahamas that turned out to be accepting bribes from a rogue CIA agent. John doxxed him and then he sailed off into the horizon.

But all of this stuff is questionable. You know, what was happening? What level of pursuit was in these places while John was out in the boat, it's questionable. You just need to look at the footage. Robert King's footage. It was madness. It was drug-fuelled the whole thing. So, John's perception of what might have been happening and what was happening might be two different things.

WHACKD – In June 2019, John claimed on Twitter that he had 31 terabytes of incriminating data on world governments. What are your thoughts or comments on that?

Mark Eglinton – No, I never believed it. He said it to me, and I asked him what it was, but he deflected. This became the dead-mans-switch theory, which everyone got excited about after his death. I personally never believed it.

I think it's a bit like the doxxing the guy in the Bahamas, Paul Rolle, his name was. He was the Bahamian police commissioner or something like that. I believe that was the extent of the kind of material John was able to get, In my opinion.

I might be surprised one day if all of a sudden, this stuff does dump out there. But I don't think it will. I think that was John's bravado. I don't think John ever had that kind of information.

WHACKD – John was later deported to London from the Dominican Republic and then went off the grid in Europe, eventually ending up in Spain. Did he share any particularly notable stories from that time?

Mark Eglinton – Now, he was only in London because of his dual citizenship passport, he didn't want to go back to the US. He knew that he was in trouble in the US. He thought that from London he could probably get out into the rest of Europe, and he did.

He told me a story about when he was in London, he went to some event there and some woman tried to flip a hotel room key in his pocket, he thought it was some girl who fancied him but it wasn't it was somebody contracted to try and pick him up.

These things did seem to happen to John. I don't know exactly where he went from London or how he ended up in Spain, the time between these two times is still unclear to me. should say, I didn't know John was in Spain when I was talking to him. I found that out later because he never told me. I had kind of worked it out because of the time of day that I was speaking to him and I could tell that he was by the sea. It looked Mediterranean. I mean, I'd figured out it was probably somewhere in southern France, Spain, Italy, or somewhere like that but I don't know how he got there, and I don't know what happened between London and Spain.

WHACKD – John was later imprisoned by the Spanish authorities after his passport was flagged. Can you provide more detail about that time?

Mark Eglinton – Well, this was at the time that I had decided to do the book by myself, we had kind of finished talking but there was still some dialogue back and forth. I could tell whenever I was engaging with John by email that he was tense. Something was going on, I could tell by the demeanour I mean, I could read into the words. There was real pressure.

There were a couple of times when we were working too where John would kind of throw me off and say something like "Right I'm flying to Ukraine" or Norway, it was like "I'll be back on such and such." I wasn't convinced. I don't know if he made these trips or whether these were just his decoys or misinformation games.

I could be wrong here, but I do believe Janice has said that John freely flew around Europe before being picked up on that passport, I don't know if that's true or not. All I do know is that he was flying to Istanbul at the time of his arrest. I don't know why. I'd never asked him, and I never got the chance to ask him, but that's what he was doing. They wanted to extradite him, it's not very complicated to have somebody's details flagged by airport security when they come through, but that's all I know about that.

WHACKD – Did you have any communication with John whilst he was imprisoned?

Mark Eglinton – Yeah, I had a bit of communication with John through Janice. I told Janice when the book deal had been done when it was coming out and to pass that news on to John. The message came back from John that he was looking forward to reading the book when it came out, so that was all good.

I did try to send quite a few packages to John whilst he was in prison, letters, a couple of books, stuff like that, stuff that we talked about. But it all came back, which was weird. I got all the details for the prison in Spain from Janice, the exact address, postcode, and things like that. I know it was correct but everything came back about a month after I sent it. Not even opened.

This stuff was just fired straight back. Well, was that by the Spanish mail service? Or the prison? It wouldn't be John. He would have wanted it, but nothing got through.

WHACKD – Can you remember the details of your final conversation with John? Are you able to share that?

Mark Eglinton – The final spoken conversation would have been about the end of the book deal, about how the previous book deal fell apart. It wasn't very pleasant. It felt kind of bittersweet. I felt like he screwed me over, I've never really said that before, I thought to introduce the crypto stuff and the address stuff at the final hurdle, I thought it kind of sabotaged something.

There was a while when I wondered whether he did that intentionally. Was it just a reason to throw a spanner in the works? I wondered if that when it came to it, John didn't want this side of him out there. That's what I wondered, it wasn't the case, but it's what I wondered at that time. It was a bit unpleasant, it wasn't like "fuck you then," It was just disappointing and he was like "I'm sorry you feel that way."

It developed from there and we continued to communicate. We always communicated on Skype for some unknown reason, Skype direct message. I don't communicate with anyone else on Skype, but that's what we used. I've still got all these messages stretching back over a long period. There's probably a book to be written of that itself. That whole Skype dialogue, some of it is bizarre, but I think the last communication I had with him was about a month before he was arrested. I went back to check some detail that I wanted to put in the book about something, I can't even remember what it was now. I wish I had something more dramatic, but it wasn't like that. It was just something mundane. You know, on this day did this happen then and he was like, "Yeah, you got that right." So, that's what it was.

WHACKD – On June 23rd of 2021, it was reported that John commits suicide in jail. What did you make of that? Do you believe John was WHACKD?

Mark Eglinton – I've been through a couple of different iterations of thought over time. Initially, I thought it was possible that someone could have had him killed, I was always a little suspicious. People said it couldn't be suicide because John was larger than life, or that he enjoyed living. He did. There's no doubt about that. But was also John being 74, was an ultra-realist.

This goes back to the two sides sort of John I spoke of earlier. John could be upbeat but he could also be pretty down and depressed. I could easily see a situation where John just thought "Fuck It, I've had enough." Not many other people know John well enough to recognise that he could do that.

The longer it went on, I started thinking that I don't know why someone would have him killed. I can't think of a reason. You know, particularly when I've dismissed the whole dead-mans-switch thing. I never bought into that.

So, for me, it was never like, 'Oh, he's got all this information that you know, somebody could have been killed for that.' That's just my opinion. I could be wrong and if I am, so be it. But my conclusion is that I think it's more likely that he is still alive than it is that somebody killed him.

I had this conversation with Robert King the other day. You know, if somebody told me 'Oh by the way John McAfee is alive living in Mongolia, under a pseudonym.' I actually wouldn't be that surprised. I wouldn't be shocked if anybody could have pulled it off John could. But I think the reality is probably a bit sadder and a bit more boring. I think he might have just committed suicide. Again, just my opinion, and I'm only going on my feelings.

WHACKD – Are you able to speak on Janice's current situation in Spain with the authorities still withholding John's remains?

Mark Eglinton – I can speak on it; I just can't give you any answers. I mean, I don't understand how she can be in Spain without a visa for two years. I don't understand who's paying for her to be there, or paying her legal fees. I don't understand that. I don't know if she's under duress of any kind. Is there anyone deciding what she's doing? I just don't know. It's all a mystery.

I'm in touch with Janice quite a lot, a little less than I used to be, but I check in with her once in a while. She goes through peaks and troughs, upbeat sometimes then depressed other times. It's understandable given her situation. But I have no idea what the end game is here. I just don't know what's going to happen.

I said to Robert King the other day, "We could be two years on here, two years with his body still there. You know, then what? Five? Ten? I mean, where's this going to go?" I don't know. I don't know if Janice knows that either. But I can't help thinking that she's in Spain for a specific reason, I don't know what that reason is.

WHACKD – Your recordings with John have been optioned to Amanda Milius for a potential movie in pre-production titled 'WHACKD.' Can you share any more details about that?

Mark Eglinton – Yeah, I mean, I had no plans to do this. I was doing an interview on Steve Bannon's 'War Room', he was a big champion of McAfee and liked him and all that kind of stuff and so he got me on there and Amanda was on as well, nothing to do with my stuff, she was on for something else and Steve just brought it up and he said "You should make a movie about McAfee" and she said "okay, cool" and that's pretty much what's happened.

I had no expectation or real understanding of what would be involved but I agreed to do it and I signed the deal which encompassed the book and the audio for a set period. The way options work is that they take it for some time and then they either extend it or they don't, they either make a movie or they don't. That's pretty much where it's at.

The whole point of doing something like that for someone like me is that I don't get involved in the day-to-day conversation. I'm a consultant as and when needed, I should say that I'm a little bit in the dark as to what's happening and that's a disappointment from the perspective of the momentum. I felt the momentum was there to make it happen sooner than it has. For obvious reasons, not just that other movies were coming out but that people just forget.

WHACKD – During the time that you got to know John, did he change your outlook or perspective in any particular way? And if so, how?

Mark Eglinton – Yeah, good question. The easy thing to say is that John made you feel like you should live your life more, and that's true, he did. But honestly, I'd kind of gone through that myself already some years before, trying to escape the matrix when it comes to work. I'd done that ten years before meeting John McAfee I had decided I wasn't working for anyone else, I'm unemployable, all that stuff, but John reaffirmed that, he was 25 years older than me. He reaffirmed what I already knew: don't waste your time on arguments. That was one thing that resonated with me.

John was kind of like a father figure because he would forewarn me and tell me about things that I'd probably discover in the next 25 years, and that's valuable. I didn't have that kind of relationship with my father. My father was one of these pretty stoic Scottish, working-class guys who certainly didn't talk about any bigger issues in the world. It was a very sort of micro-life type thing and that's okay. That's how he lived.

But John introduced me to a much bigger world and reaffirmed that you know, life is for living. But, as I said, I'd already reached that point myself, but John made it clearer.

WHACKD – What does John McAfee's legacy mean to you and how will he be remembered in your mind?

Mark Eglinton – Oh, God. I'm just trying to articulate this. Well, this applies to whomever you work with. I always acknowledge that once you work with someone whether it's a footballer like Michael Owen or an entrepreneur like McAfee, a lawyer, or whomever the hell it is: Whether you like it or not, your lives are intertwined. If you get along with them then it's a good time. If you don't get on with someone then it's tough shit. Your lives are still intertwined.

With John, it's the same, particularly given what has happened since. It's something that I'll never really be able to escape and I don't know if I would ever really want to escape it. I don't want it to go away. I don't want to say oh, forget the whole McAfee years in my life. however long they were or are, I don't want to do that. This is a part of my life.

I think about John, probably every day one way or the other. I'm not sitting around pining about what happened to him or going too deep into the weeds about what the situation might be, but he enters my mind and I think that'll always be the case. I don't think you can escape these things, particularly when you've been involved with someone in the way that I was. Many people have been close to John over the years but I think I was in a unique position in terms of the time in his life that we met.

He was in a situation where he wanted his story told, he was in a situation where he knew his life was under threat and time was probably running out. He saw me as the vehicle to get it out there.

We used each other. We both acknowledged that very early on. He said, "I'm using you." And I said "Well, I'm using you too" because let's not kid ourselves doing this was going to elevate my credibility and he knew that when I got the book out there it would elevate his story.

We had a mutual understanding and that's how it will always be. I'll always view him fondly; I don't know if that'll change if anything dramatic happens. If he's found to be alive somewhere in Mongolia, I don't know how that could change but as it stands John will always be a part of my life, like many others, but probably a little bit more special to me than others.

WHACKD – Do you have any other thoughts or comments to share before we wrap this up?

Mark Eglinton – I think the world John put out there in interviews on YouTube and stuff was this sort of macro show world. Whereas the world that we had discussed was much more kind of an inner world. You know, feelings and stuff. You couldn't get John to talk about these things in a YouTube interview because he switched to a different persona. But with me, it was a different thing.

There are gaps in my conversations with John that people are always hoping I can fill in, it just is what it is. Most of what we talked about are in the book. The rest that isn't in the book is in the audio, which hopefully will come out in a movie when it happens.

WHACKD – We will end it here, thank you for doing this.

Closing Acknowledgements

Thank you for reading "In Memoriam: McAfee Remembered". The homage to John McAfee's extraordinary life and a solace for those who mourn him. We express our sincere gratitude to John's friends, family and business partners, for trusting us with their personal stories and memories. We hope that this book honours their relationship with the late tech pioneer.

We acknowledge that John was a controversial and divisive figure. He faced many accusations and criticisms throughout his life, some of which were never resolved or proven. He also had many enemies and detractors who wanted to harm or discredit him. We do not claim to have the final word on John's truth or innocence.

We have tried to present his story as objectively and fairly as possible, based on the first-hand testimonies of those closest to him while portraying his human side, his strengths and weaknesses, his successes and failures, and his joys and sorrows. We hope that this book will inspire more research and discussion on John's legacy and impact.

Whether you respected, opposed, or were simply intrigued by him, we hope that you have learned something new and take something valuable from his story. John McAfee was not a flawless man, but he was a remarkable one. He never backed down from his beliefs, even when they had serious consequences, his death is a testament to that fact.

John David McAfee was a man who walked his talk and carved out his own path, leaving an indelible mark on the world. We believe that his courage, spirit, and determination will continue to inspire those who recognize that influence within themselves.

Rest in peace, John. Your wild and beautiful soul will never be forgotten.

www.ingramcontent.com/pod-product-compliance
Lightning Source LLC
Chambersburg PA
CBHW022140050726
47590CB00002B/517